Cambridge Elements

Elements in Public Engagement with Science
edited by
Angela Potochnik
University of Cincinnati
Melissa Jacquart
University of Cincinnati

PUBLIC ENGAGEMENT WITH SCIENCE

Defining the Project

Angela Potochnik
University of Cincinnati

Melissa Jacquart
University of Cincinnati

Shaftesbury Road, Cambridge CB2 8EA, United Kingdom

One Liberty Plaza, 20th Floor, New York, NY 10006, USA

477 Williamstown Road, Port Melbourne, VIC 3207, Australia

314–321, 3rd Floor, Plot 3, Splendor Forum, Jasola District Centre,
New Delhi – 110025, India

103 Penang Road, #05–06/07, Visioncrest Commercial, Singapore 238467

Cambridge University Press is part of Cambridge University Press & Assessment,
a department of the University of Cambridge.

We share the University's mission to contribute to society through the pursuit of
education, learning and research at the highest international levels of excellence.

www.cambridge.org
Information on this title: www.cambridge.org/9781009475129
DOI: 10.1017/9781009475105

© Angela Potochnik and Melissa Jacquart 2025

This publication is in copyright. Subject to statutory exception and to the provisions of relevant collective licensing agreements, with the exception of the Creative Commons version the link for which is provided below, no reproduction of any part may take place without the written permission of Cambridge University Press & Assessment.

An online version of this work is published at doi.org/10.1017/9781009475105 under a Creative Commons Open Access license CC-BY-NC-ND 4.0 which permits re-use, distribution and reproduction in any medium for noncommercial purposes providing appropriate credit to the original work is given. You may not distribute derivative works without permission. To view a copy of this license, visit https://creativecommons.org/licenses/by-nc-nd/4.0

When citing this work, please include a reference to the DOI 10.1017/9781009475105

First published 2025

A catalogue record for this publication is available from the British Library

ISBN 978-1-009-47512-9 Hardback
ISBN 978-1-009-47511-2 Paperback
ISSN 2753-7137 (online)
ISSN 2753-7129 (print)

Cambridge University Press & Assessment has no responsibility for the persistence or accuracy of URLs for external or third-party internet websites referred to in this publication and does not guarantee that any content on such websites is, or will remain, accurate or appropriate.

For EU product safety concerns, contact us at Calle de José Abascal, 56, 1°, 28003 Madrid, Spain, or email eugpsr@cambridge.org.

Public Engagement with Science

Defining the Project

Elements in Public Engagement with Science

DOI: 10.1017/9781009475105
First published online: January 2025

Angela Potochnik
University of Cincinnati

Melissa Jacquart
University of Cincinnati

Author for correspondence: Angela Potochnik, angela.potochnik@uc.edu

Abstract: "Public engagement with science" is gaining currency as the framing for outreach activities related to science. However, knowledge bearing on the topic is siloed in a variety of disciplines, and public engagement activities often are conducted without support from relevant theory or familiarity with related activities. This first Element in the Public Engagement with Science series sets the stage for the series by delineating the target of investigation, establishing the importance of cross-disciplinary collaboration and community partnerships for effective public engagement with science, examining the roles public engagement with science plays in academic institutions, and providing initial resources for the theory and practice of public engagement with science. This is useful to academics who would like to conduct or study public engagement with science, as well as to public engagement practitioners as a window into relevant academic knowledge and cultures. This title is also available as open access on Cambridge Core.

Keywords: public engagement with science, science education, science communication, science policy, public understanding of science, museum studies, science and technology studies, philosophy of science

© Angela Potochnik and Melissa Jacquart

ISBNs: 9781009475129 (HB), 9781009475112 (PB), 9781009475105 (OC)
ISSNs: 2753-7137 (online), 2753-7129 (print)

Contents

1 What Is Public Engagement with Science?   1

2 Disciplinary Expertise Bearing on Public Engagement with Science   19

3 An Essentially Collaborative Endeavor   32

4 Goals and Goal-Directed Design   50

5 Conducting, Teaching, and Researching Public Engagement with Science   70

Appendix: Guide for Designing a Public Engagement with Science Initiative   80

References   82

1 What Is Public Engagement with Science?

Just about everyone interacts with the products of science every day: the medicines we take, the technologies we rely on, and the very methods we use to learn about the world around us are all deeply influenced by science. Science is viewed as so valuable that science education is a core component of education curricula the world over. Arguably, science is the predominant framework through which Western societies understand our experience of the world, and it guides our decisions about how we structure society through public policy. It makes sense, therefore, that scientific literacy, public trust in scientific institutions, and policies based on science are all generally seen to be of societal value.

However, people's relationships to science vary. Not everyone has the same depth of understanding of scientific findings. And not everyone places a high value on science. How the public feels about and relates to science has received increasing attention and even advocacy in recent years. For example, in 2017, March for Science events held around the world aimed to emphasize how science is a common good and advocated for evidence-based, science-informed public policies. More recently, international responses to the Covid-19 pandemic served as a stark reminder of the need for broad-based scientific literacy, trust in scientific institutions, and science-informed policies and practices.

For these reasons, scientists and other academics are increasingly called upon to not only conduct research but also to engage in public outreach. Scientific funding agencies expect grantees to not only pursue research of high intellectual merit but also to engage in meaningful societal broader impacts (as with the US's National Science Foundation) or knowledge mobilization or translation (for Canada's National Research Council and the European Research Council) related to their research. Furthermore, many scientists find employment outside the academy in roles that relate to public outreach. STEM workforce development and STEM education have also received sustained attention and significant governmental and philanthropic financial investment. A wide range of professional roles exist at the interface between science and the public, such as science educators, museum curators, science communicators, science journalists, science policy experts, and more.

All of this is a testament to the importance of the relationship between science and the public as a topic of research, to the permeability of the academic/professional boundary with regards to public engagement with science, and to the topic's inherent interdisciplinarity. Research bearing on public engagement with science is conducted in a range of disciplines including communication, education, museum studies, philosophy of science, political science, social and community psychology, science and technology studies, educational research based in individual scientific disciplines, and more. Further, public engagement with science professionals – educators, curators, science communicators, journalists, policymakers, etc. – have developed bodies of expertise that shape their work. Yet, at present, it is nearly impossible for a researcher or outreach practitioner to navigate this research, distributed as it is across disciplines and influenced by different research traditions, and to access the variety of relevant professional expertise.

This Element is the first in an interdisciplinary series, *Cambridge Elements in Public Engagement with Science*, that will draw from expertise and research findings in a range of disciplines and professions, developing those insights into forms with which academics and professionals from a variety of backgrounds can effectively engage. In this Element, we set the stage for this initiative by characterizing public engagement with science as a target of inquiry, describing some of the academic disciplines that bear on its study and practice, and outlining broad contours of effective theory, methods, and practice related to public engagement with science. This Element is perhaps most useful to academics who conduct or are interested in conducting public engagement activities or who carry out research on public engagement with science. But, we hope it is also useful to public engagement practitioners as a window into relevant academic knowledge and cultures.

This first section begins the project by offering an initial characterization of public engagement with science. In Section 1.1, we explore the many interfaces between science and the public and offer an initial definition of public engagement with science. This definition is expanded and clarified through the remainder of the introduction. In Sections 1.2 and 1.3, we explore the aims public engagement with science can have. That discussion begins in Section 1.2 with the widely appreciated aim of increased public understanding of science, and then Section 1.3 considers other, distinct aims for public engagement with science, including developing public trust of science, increasing public access to scientific participation and findings, and cultivating social and personal identities related to science. In Section 1.4, we consider how public engagement with science involves not merely one-way influence of academic science on the public but instead multidirectional influence between science and the public. Section 1.5 concludes the introduction by outlining the contents of the remainder of the Element.

1.1 Science in the Public Sphere

In contemporary society, scientific research directly or indirectly impacts nearly everyone's life. This occurs through daily comforts and conveniences, technological and virtual tools, medical care and treatments, and more. Most also encounter required science education in their schooling. Science is, in some sense, inescapable. Yet different segments of the public have very different relationships to science. Some have careers related to science; just over 6 percent of the United States workforce, for instance, is employed in STEM careers (Fry et al., 2021) while in the UK, STEM careers are estimated to be 8.5 percent of the workforce (Science and Technology Committee, 2023). Some are science enthusiasts or have hobbies related to science, likely including the 1.07 million estimated participants worldwide in the inaugural March for Science in 2017, and many more people besides. Others may have only taken the required science classes during their schooling, and some may have disliked or failed those classes. And still others – some of whom know quite a bit about science – distrust the scientific enterprise in its entirety or particular segments of it, such as climate change research, evolutionary theory, vaccination, pharmaceutical research, or agricultural technology.

A person's relationship with science also intersects with other aspects of their social and cultural identity. For example, the PEW Research Center (Fry et al., 2021) and National Science Board (Burke et al., 2022) report that Black and Hispanic workers in the US remain underrepresented in STEM careers compared to other jobs. Women, meanwhile, are underrepresented in computing and engineering, while they make up a majority of the health-related workforce. And, while the number of STEM degrees is increasing more than overall degrees earned, Black and Hispanic students remain underrepresented in most STEM degree programs, and women remain underrepresented in some of these programs, especially computer science and engineering (Fry et al., 2021). In addition to race/ethnicity and gender, a person's educational level also correlates with their relationship with science. Those who do not attend college are limited in their exposure to science education and their participation in STEM careers. Further, distrust of science is also shaped by political identity and racial and ethnic identity. For example, in the US, trust in scientists is higher among Democrats than Republicans and trust in medical scientists is higher among White adults than Black adults (Funk et al., 2020).

How the public – and different segments of the public – relate to science is at the heart of how we understand public engagement with science. For the purposes of this Element, and the ensuing series, we define this as follows:

> **Public engagement with science:** attempts to intervene on some aspect(s) of how some segment of the public relates to science, to the end of improving the relationship

Notice first that this is more than a project of *describing* how the public or some segment thereof relates to science. Public engagement with science, as we use the term here, involves someone attempting to change something about the relationships between science and the public for the better, that is, to improve it along one dimension or another. Of course, ideas of what constitutes an improvement vary. It is also important to note that the public is not homogeneous, and conducting public engagement with science almost invariably involves a particular segment of the public, distinguished by nationality, geographic location, age group, educational level, and/or other variables. The question of what about the public's relationship to science should be targeted in public engagement with science initiatives is a matter of extensive discussion and research. This will emerge as an important theme in this section and in the Element as a whole. Further, public engagement with science efforts may be more or less systematic, theory-driven, or ad hoc. Public engagement with science also may occur as part of academic or institutional science or in public spaces, driven by community organizations or community members themselves.

Defined this broadly, public engagement with science can take many forms. One example is an academic scientist giving a public talk about their research or responding to press inquiries. Another is a science fair for middle-school students. Public engagement with science can also consist in public involvement in scientific or medical research, as with citizen science or community-based participatory research, or even community efforts to spur scientific research on a matter they deem important. Because the relationships between science and the public are so extensive, public engagement with science can take many forms and also vary in who leads the engagement. Because those relationships are so variable, public engagement with science can target many types of people and have many different goals. We will explore these varying features of public engagement with science – aims it might have, forms it can take, who might conduct it, and who it might target – later in this section and throughout the rest of this Element. We will also characterize some main types of public engagement with science activities in Section 5.

The American Association for the Advancement of Science (AAAS) (https://www.aaas.org), the world's largest multidisciplinary scientific society, defines public engagement with science as "intentional, meaningful interactions that provide opportunities for mutual learning between scientists and members of the public" (AAAS, 2016). Our definition shares this definition's focus on intervention, but our definition does not specify a focus on learning. Public engagement with science, as we understand it, may target a number of different features of the public's relationship to science. The AAAS definition also specifies *mutual* learning. We agree that public engagement with science should often involve bidirectional or multidirectional influence among the parties. But rather than define public engagement with science as including bidirectional influence at this stage, we will explore how this is a feature of the productive pursuit of public engagement with science later in the section.

1.2 Public Understanding of Science

Given the broad way we've defined public engagement with science, the many relationships between science and the public, and the different ways different segments of the public tend to relate to science, there is a question of what features of the public's relationship to science should be a focal point for public engagement with science. What is important about how the public relates to science?

Despite our insistence that the aims of public engagement with science may include something other than education, a focus on public understanding of science is a natural starting point for a discussion of the aims of public engagement with science. Indeed, a common focus of public engagement with science is improving scientific literacy, that is, knowledge or understanding of scientific findings and practices.[1] The depth of public understanding of science in the US has been surveyed every two years since the 1950s through the National Science Board's Science & Technology Indicators (https://ncses.nsf.gov/pubs/nsb20221), prepared by the National Science Foundation's National Center for Science and Engineering Statistics, and in Great Britain since 1988 (Miller, 2001; NASEM, 2016). Further, the Organization for Economic Cooperation and Development (OECD) has assessed scientific literacy across the world every three years since 2006.

Science is typically an explicit priority in formal education, even if it arguably should receive more dedicated attention than it does. Most people around the world encounter science courses during their education. In many nations, science courses are required during childhood education, and many universities require their students to take one or more science courses as well. Further, in some nations, teaching standards for science education receive significant attention. Beyond its role in formal education, scientific literacy is also frequently targeted in informal education in museums, libraries, after-school activities, and other settings. Scientific literacy or understanding is generally taken to consist in mastery of scientific content, methods, and practices. These are the focus of the OECD and other assessments mentioned just above. These are also prioritized in educational standards, such as the US's Next Generation

---

[1] This initial characterization sidesteps significant controversy about how scientific literacy should be defined and the nature of its value; see for instance (Pardo and Calvo, 2004; Feinstein, 2011; Roberts and Bybee, 2014; Keren, 2018). Some of this controversy will be signaled below, but it is beyond the scope of this Element to survey and establish a position on how scientific literacy should be defined.

Science Standards (NGSS), which include three "dimensions": disciplinary core ideas, science and engineering practices, and cross-cutting concepts (NGSS, 2017).

Just as surveys of scientific literacy and science educational standards focus primarily on knowledge of scientific content, so too is scientific-content knowledge sometimes taken to be the goal of public engagement with science. The aim of a museum visit, public lecture, or magazine article can be conveying a clearer sense for what we have come to understand about the world through scientific research. And yet, conveying knowledge of scientific content need not be the main focus of increasing scientific understanding. For instance, Feinstein (2011) criticizes a lack of attention in the study of scientific literacy to the question of how deeper scientific understanding is of value to the (nonscientist) public. He suggests that the aim of public understanding of science should not be to help the public to understand the same things as scientists but rather to cultivate "competent outsiders" who can identify when science is a relevant resource for addressing their goals and effectively bring scientific expertise to bear in those circumstances (see also Kampourakis, 2022). In Feinstein's view, this aim of scientific literacy is best supported by enabling the situation-specific use of others' scientific expertise rather than the cultivation of one's own wide-ranging expertise in science. This calls into question the centrality of scientific-content knowledge to public understanding of science. At the very least, this broadened target for public understanding of science makes salient the questions of, first, what segments of the public are targeted in efforts to increase public understanding of science and, second, what specific goal(s) for these segments of the public is served by increasing scientific understanding.

Increasingly, informal science education practitioners attend to questions like these. In contrast to scientific-content knowledge, improved public understanding of scientific methods and practices can be useful to cultivating "competent outsiders" to science. This is because the methods and practices of science are crucial to science's expertise and help provide guidance about why and when to seek scientific expertise. A better grasp of scientific methods and practices can help members of the public indirectly assess scientific findings for themselves. For example, nonscientists may not need to know how to use statistics to test a hypothesis, but nonscientists do benefit from knowing about how statistical hypothesis-testing extends the reach of conclusions scientists can draw, and about how variation means we can't draw firm conclusions about the world based only on salient examples we know about (such as the grandpa who smoked like a chimney but lived to see his 100th birthday).

A focus on how scientific literacy can produce "competent outsiders" to science also motivates a special focus on evaluating scientific expertise.

Insiders to science – scientists, technicians, and medical professionals – need a solid working knowledge of scientific findings, methods, and practice relevant to their work. The nonscientist public, in contrast, might be better served by a nuanced understanding of how to identify and assess scientific expertise: who is an expert, about what, and the role of scientific consensus in establishing trustworthy knowledge (Feinstein, 2011; Keren, 2018; see also Potochnik, 2024, for additional discussion). So, even when public engagement focuses on the aim of improved public understanding, there are rich questions to ask about what should be understood, and why. There's also a question of whether communities might be a better target for scientific understanding than individuals (NASEM, 2016).

Beyond the question of what the goals of public understanding of science should be, there is also a question of how this understanding – whether of scientific-content knowledge, methods, practices, or expertise – can best be achieved. We will address this question more fully later in the Element, when we look at effective design of public engagement with science initiatives. For now, we will start by pointing out that a commonly employed approach of simply sharing scientific knowledge with the public is not as effective in achieving understanding as one might expect it to be. This is widely called the "deficit model" of scientific understanding, as it presumes the public has a knowledge deficit that scientists can simply fill (Wynne, 1991; Ziman, 1991; Layton, 1993). Goals in line with the deficit model, like better informing the public or countering misinformation, are common for scientists and other academics to prioritize, but communication research has shown this approach to be ineffective (Besley et al., 2015; Simis et al., 2016). Instead, as with any education, public understanding of science requires proper orientation to the content, aligned motivations, and active synthesis.

This is one shortcoming of the deficit model: coming to understand involves much more than simply uptake of information. Another shortcoming of the deficit model relates to the very *aim* of public engagement. Increased understanding is not always the only or the most important aim of public engagement. We noted above that factors such as political affiliation and race are correlated with propensity to trust scientists. This hints at how social identities can be relevant to one's relationship to science.

In a 2015 study, the Pew Research Center surveyed US adults and members of the AAAS (American Association for the Advancement of Science, the multidisciplinary science society mentioned above). The results indicated large gaps between members of the AAAS and the broader public in their views on some key topics of scientific research. For example, 88% of AAAS members judged genetically modified foods to be safe, while only 37% of the broader public did. 98% of AAAS members agree that humans have evolved over time, while only 65% of the broader public agrees with this claim (Pew Research Center, 2015). See the interactive graphic at https://www.pewre search.org/internet/interactives/public-scientists-opinion-gap/ for a depiction of more of the gaps in views.

Initially, this seems to suggest that there is a gap in public understanding of these topics compared to scientific understanding. But things might not be so simple. Kahan (2017) examined public responses to the National Science Foundation's longstanding survey of scientific understanding. Two of the largest gaps in public understanding revealed in that survey regarded evolution and the big bang theory of the formation of the universe. Kahan found that slight modifications to the questions – swapping out humans with elephants as the topic of the evolution question and asking not what the survey participant believes about the universe's formation but what scientists believe – significantly lessened the gap between public opinion and scientific consensus. Crucially, neither of those changes to wording altered the knowledge needed to answer correctly. Instead, they simply changed the valence of these questions about these topics, both of which are of significant social controversy. This raises the question of whether the gap in opinions between scientists and the broader public always relates to differences in knowledge. It seems elements of identity and social affinities might influence these differences in view.[2]

1.3 Additional Aims of Public Engagement with Science

Increased understanding of science isn't always the route to an improved relationship with science. For one thing, features of one's social and personal identity can play an important role in one's tendency to accept science's authority, seek scientific insight, or even be interested in science. Research has shown that knowledge of a scientific issue and attitudes toward the issue are only weakly related, and for some topics, more scientific knowledge predicts either strong acceptance or strong denial (Allum et al., 2008). For example, increased knowledge of climate science is associated with the polarization of beliefs about climate change (Weisberg et al., 2018).

So, while improved scientific understanding may be part of what is targeted in public engagement with science, this is often not the only relevant aim.[3]

---

[2] See (McCain and Kampourakis, 2018; Metz et al., 2020; Weisberg et al., 2021) for additional discussion of polling about beliefs on evolution.
[3] In this Element, we use "aim" to refer to a broad targeted outcome of engagement, such as promoting understanding. We use "goal" to refer to a more specific targeted outcome of engagement, such as helping museum guests to better understand the evidence for blackholes (for example).

Research suggests that aspects of personal and social identity or values are also important (see for example Kahan et al., 2011; Landrum (2020) is a video that is a particularly useful resource in exploring this point). This is so especially when a topic is politically charged or otherwise bound up with identity. For instance, views about science in the US are correlated both with an individual's generation and political party affiliation (Pew Research Center, 2021). The relationship between views about science and personal and social identity may thus be relevant to the aims of public engagement with science initiatives. Initiatives may target segments of the public with specific relevant identities, may be tailored to be effective with particular social identities, or may even aim to influence how science is interpreted as relating to relevant personal or social identities.

Also bound up with social identity is trust in science: members of the public may be hesitant to trust scientists and scientific findings. Some sources of distrust include when public confidence in scientific institutions and government bodies has been shaken by fraud, research scandals, and misconduct – or the appearance of them. Scientists historically have used some communities to produce scientific advances with little regard for these communities' rights and needs. Prime examples include communities of color and colonized nations; perhaps the most common example cited is the 40-year Tuskegee Untreated Syphilis Study and increase in medical mistrust by Black men (Alsan and Wanamaker, 2018). Such instances unethical scientific research led to the 1978 Belmont Report and resulting creation in the US of the Office for Human Research Protections (OHRP), as well as laws requiring institutional review board approval for any scientific studies involving human subjects. While review boards aim to provide ethical checks, there is still warranted mistrust by communities due to these histories.

Presently, mistrust of science associated with some political or religious identities has given rise to a phenomenon known as "science denial." Science denial is rejecting scientific findings that, according to the norms of science, should be accepted. Rejected findings tend to be viewed as incompatible with salient political or religious commitments, such as evolution, especially of humans, the "big bang" origin of the universe, the safety of some or all vaccines, and, perhaps most notably, human-caused climate change. A step beyond denial of specific scientific findings is using that distrust in a specific scientific finding one objects to as a reason to doubt the whole scientific enterprise (McIntyre, 2021). Political valence in the patterns of science denial and reactions to it has led to the increasing political polarization of science itself in the US, that is, an association of science with the political left and as opposed to the political right.

Public engagement with science initiatives should be developed with awareness of the possibility of encountering mistrust of science, including distrust resulting from past injustices, and some public engagement initiatives may aim to ameliorate distrust or enhance the trustworthiness or appearance of trustworthiness of scientific institutions. Yet, there is need for public engagement initiatives, especially those led by scientists, to focus more on aims related to trust than they typically do. As the AAAS report notes,

> There is a clear gap between research showing the importance of trust, and scientists' perceptions of what is important in outreach or engagement efforts. Research shows that scientists least prioritize communication goals and training opportunities that focus on trust-building (Besley et al., 2015; AAAS, 2016).

Philosopher and historian of science Maya Goldenberg (2021) has encouraged a shift in framing from seeing science denial as a war on the expertise of science to seeing it instead as a crisis of trust in science and medicine. This reframing draws attention away from criticizing individuals who deny scientific expertise or scientific findings, like climate change and the safety of vaccinations, and toward working to develop trust in science and medicine. For example, in the case of medicine, one might focus on trust-building through means like patient–doctor relationships. Misinformation on social media certainly isn't helping the situation, but if people had better access to scientific expertise and a better understanding of why and when science is trustworthy, then they would be less easy targets for misinformation. This need offers a particularly good opportunity for the development of public engagement with science initiatives. Similarly, philosophers de Melo-Martín and Intemann (2018) point to enhancing the trustworthiness of scientific community as a more useful approach (especially for biomedical and environmental sciences, and when tackling inappropriate cases of dissent).

So far, then, we've surveyed three possible aims of public engagement with science: increasing scientific understanding, influencing how science relates to personal and social identities, and increasing trust in science. Beyond these, another possible aim for public engagement with science initiatives is improving access to science in one way or another. This might include healthcare access. Geographic location, for example, may preclude certain segments of the public from having a hospital or clinic nearby offering the services they need. Or, this might involve increasing the access of rural communities to informal educational experiences, such as offered by museums or zoos, to better match the opportunities of urban communities. Increasing access to science might also take the form of improved access to scientific knowledge or research, such as targeted research on a local environmental concern, as with community-led environmental or water safety research. Or the aim of increased access might focus on inclusion in the STEM workforce. There is a long history of some identities, such as women, racial and ethnic minorities, persons with disabilities, and members of the LGBTQIA community, being excluded from the STEM workforce (see National Academies' summary reports from 2006, 2011, 2017 for discussion). Public engagement with science thus may aim at improving access to STEM careers for people with one or more of these identities via helping to foster a sense of belonging in STEM (Rainey et al., 2018).

Finally, one further possible aim of public engagement with science relates to demonstrating science's value or applying science in a way that is useful. Some public engagement with science initiatives may simply aim to help the public to see the instrumental value of science. Some members of the public may not be interested in science beyond the ways in which it can help their lives, such as through health or technological advancements. Another sense in which science might have instrumental value is in supporting the use of scientific tools, regardless of whether the public participants come to know how those tools work. Consider, for example, an activity in which test strips are used to test levels of lead in drinking water or using GPS for a geocaching activity. One does not need to know the science behind how these tools work to benefit from seeing their effective use and, in some cases, what is learned through their use. In this case, the benefit is not so much a greater understanding of science but a greater appreciation for ways in which scientific tools can be valuable and the gain of practical benefit through the use of those tools. Another instrumental use of science in public engagement occurs in science policy. Science policy involves the uptake of scientific findings and the application of scientific tools to influence social policy. In this context, it is not how the public comes to regard or relate to science that is key, but how scientific tools and findings are put to work for public good.

While promoting the value of science because of the benefits it offers is one version of the aim of demonstrating science's value, another version might focus on developing an appreciation for science in and of itself – for enjoyment or fun. For example, someone might enjoy watching a nature documentary, even if they don't learn any new scientific facts from it. Likewise, a young child might visit a science museum or participate in a science booth event at a local market and come away simply with a sense of having enjoyed themselves. A legitimate aim for public engagement with science initiatives thus is participants walking away from the experience with positive feelings because they had fun. This may not involve them learning something new about the subject or having a shift in their trust or interest, though these may be additional benefits!

And, if not, enjoyment of science activities can be a first step to accessing other positive experiences with science at later junctures.

These different aims for public engagement with science – influencing understanding, identity, trust, access, and interest – are summarized in Table 1. These different aims will lead to public engagement with science initiatives with different features and priorities. Thus, an initiative focused on climate change might target, for example, public understanding of climate change impacts on sea level or public trust in climate science. Or an initiative might focus on increasing interest in how climate science can apply to predict local impacts or increasing inclusion in the sustainability workforce. Each of these types of initiative would draw on similar scientific research but would be best served by different types of engagement: targeting different segments of the public, perhaps different ages or age groupings, and involving different activities.

It's possible for these different aims to overlap and interrelate. In some cases, for example, you can't get better understanding without first increasing trust. As we have mentioned, personal and social identity can be relevant to how knowledge is acquired. Social identity can be bound up with tendency to trust or distrust science and scientific authorities. In the context of doing public engagement and outreach, even if your sole focus is increasing knowledge or understanding, you often can't avoid issues of identity and trust. And, sometimes the route to enhanced trust or shifts in identity relationships is via expanded access

Table 1 The different broad aims public engagement with science may have, as outlined in this section

Aim	Focus
Understanding	Targets understanding of scientific content, methods, and practices
Identity	Targets how personal, political, or social identities relate to science
Trust	Targets strengthening or repairing trust in science, whether distrust is due to past injustices or personal ideology
Access	Targets increasing access to goods of science, science education, or inclusion in scientific research or STEM careers
Interest: Instrumental or Intrinsic	Targets the effective application of science in day-to-day life or policy or instilling an interest in science, including simply fun or awe

and inclusion, or recognition of the instrumental usefulness or intrinsic value of science.

The five different aims for public engagement with science we've focused on here have some overlap with the six strands of science learning discussed in a National Research Council report on science learning in informal environments (NRC, 2009). We've discussed how the aim of increasing scientific understanding can have a variety of focuses including scientific content, methods, and practices, and three of the NRC strands focus on understanding: "Come to generate, understand, remember, and use concepts, explanations, arguments, models, and facts related to science" (content); "Manipulate, test, explore, predict, question, observe, and make sense of the natural and physical world" (methods); and "Reflect on science as a way of knowing; on processes, concepts, and institutions of science; and on their own process of learning about phenomena" (practices).

The fourth strand identified by the NRC report relates closely to the aim we've characterized as intrinsic interest: "Experience excitement, interest, and motivation to learn about phenomena in the natural and physical world." And their fifth strand relates closely to the aim we characterized as targeting how identities relate to science: "Think about themselves as science learners and develop an identity as someone who knows about, uses, and sometimes contributes to science." The sixth strand the NRC report identifies is "Participate in scientific activities and learning practices with others, using scientific language and tools." This focus on participation might be related to different aims: intrinsic interest or instrumental application, trust, identity, or even understanding. We thus suggest it is worth asking what the aims are for such participation. Considering overall how the NRC report's strands of science learning relate to the aims we have identified, the NRC report places relatively more emphasis on aims of understanding, including content knowledge, as well as understanding scientific practices and methods. In turn, the report does not explicitly include two aims we've highlighted: strengthening or repairing trust in science and increasing access to science goods, research, and careers.

1.4 Engagement Is Multidirectional

So far, we've defined *public engagement with science* as attempts to intervene on some aspect(s) of how some segment of the public relates to science, to the end of improving the relationship. We have also discussed how the targeted relationships may be understanding, identity, trust, access, or interest (either instrumental or intrinsic). We will round out our initial identification of public engagement with science as a target for analysis by considering how improving the relationship between science and the public can and should involve changes on both sides of that relationship.

An entryway to this idea is the discussion in Section 1.2 of the deficit model. Reincke et al. (2020), for instance, advocate replacing the one-way deficit model, which they associate with a focus on public understanding of science, with a two-way dialogue model of science communication, which they associate instead with public engagement with science. They suggest that a dialogue model adheres to three principles. First, there is explicit acknowledgment of different forms of knowledge, and that nonscientific knowledge such as cultural and experiential knowledge should be considered to have equal value as scientific knowledge. Second, scientists and nonexperts should have equal status in the conversation. Third, public engagement with science involves mutual learning, as both scientists and nonexperts learn with and from each other. The authors thus suggest that experts have three main responsibilities when implementing the dialogue model. First, they should share input and knowledge that is well received by others. Second, they should listen to and learn from the input of others. And finally, they need to invest in relationships with others. On this model, then, the central focus is not reaching consensus between scientists and nonexperts, but rather on fostering interpersonal appreciation (that is, respect and trust). Others (Simis et al., 2016; Seethaler, 2019) point toward similar sets of ethics and values for fostering effective communication that center dialectical approaches.

Understanding and other aims of engagement may not be achieved by simply disseminating information. Successful public engagement with science, even with an aim of increasing understanding, typically involves something other than just explaining scientific findings to the public. What is needed is a two-way relationship of communication. One aspect of this is that effective public engagement must be public centered in the sense that it should be shaped by the participants' interests, priorities, and needs. This is important simply for effective public engagement: calibrating what is said, or the nature of an experience, to better appeal to and address the priorities and interests of the specific public participants that are targeted. For example, a panel discussion of climate change impact may well be more engaging and effective if it focuses on local impacts of concern to the audience, such as the increased average number of heat warning days each summer in the municipality or increased extreme rains in the region, rather than generic worldwide impacts. Other features of the anticipated audience – adult-only or mixed age, climate-change advocates or broad audience, etc. – should shape the content of the panel discussion as well. (Indeed, for some audiences, such as children, a panel discussion will not be effective at all, so a different format of engagement is needed.) Further, including a robust and structured discussion will enable the panel to better respond to the audience's current state of knowledge and concerns, which are to some extent unpredictable.

So, public engagement with science benefits from bidirectionality in the sense of being shaped by the concerns of the public audiences that are engaged. But there is also another, deeper dimension of the bidirectionality of public engagement with science. Envisioning public engagement as unidirectional, with the goal merely of shifting public attitudes, is an impoverished view of what needs to change in the relationship between science and the public and of what tools are available for changing that relationship. The goal of public engagement should not be merely change in public audiences. It is equally important to reflect on the ways in which participating academics and other experts, their research and activities, and the institutions in which they participate may also be changed for the better via public engagement. This is similar to McCallie et al.'s (2009) definition of public engagement with science as "mutual learning by publics and scientists . . . in multi-directional dialogue" that "may . . . inform the direction of scientific investigations, institutions, and/or science policy."

Consider the various aims of public engagement with science detailed above. At first it might seem odd to suggest that researchers' *understanding* can be improved by public engagement; they are the experts, after all. Though public engagement is unlikely to improve researchers' subject matter expertise, this can deepen their understanding of the nature of public concerns and localized knowledge relevant to their research, how subjects they are expert in are viewed by nonexperts, and more. This knowledge can in turn enrich or clarify scientific research agendas.

For other aims of engagement, including identity, trust, access, and interest in application or enjoyment, it is even more apparent that interventions to improve these relationships between the public and science may well target the practices, participants, and institutions of science rather than simply how the public relates to science. Increased transparency of the research enterprise, for example, may improve trust more than public-focused activities designed to instill trust. Public engagement with science initiatives should proceed in a way that is sensitive to the possibility – or, in some cases, the demonstrated reality – that scientific institutions are not meeting the needs of public understanding, trust, and access. Distrust of medical science in minority communities, for example, is predicated on decades and centuries of inadequate medical care or even abuse.

Considering only changes to public attitudes is also an impoverished view of tools available for public engagement with science. The assumption that scientific research and institutions are separate from public engagement activities can lead public engagement with science to focus only on potential changes to the public. Expanding the conception of public engagement with science to include changes also to the nature of scientific research and institutions can identify new tools to shift the relationship science bears to the public, tools that may be more effective or easier to employ. For example, it may be more feasible and more effective to host public forums to consider changes to medical research at your institution and then implement some of the resulting ideas, rather than to host events for surrounding communities designed to increase their participation in medical research. Put generally, in some cases, it may be easier and more effective to change the practices of scientific institutions in ways that cultivate trust and engagement compared to directly changing public attitudes or institutions. Thus scientific research practices and institutions are worthy targets for public engagement efforts.

To summarize, public engagement with science initiatives should be developed to encourage bidirectional influence, with attention to not just how science impacts the participating public but also on how academics and other experts, their research and activities, and their institutions might shift to better fulfill their public-facing aims. In many cases, this is better described as *multi*directional influence, as there are multiple parties or institutions involved in the relationship. Scientists and the targeted public are not always or even often the only parties involved in public engagement with science initiatives. As we will discuss in Section 3, another key contributor is often community organizations that already engage with the targeted public. For example, partnership with a community organization occurs when a university researcher collaborates with a local museum or library to develop an exhibit or event for their audiences. AAAS (2016) specifies the relevant parties as scientists, publics, and practitioners; this captures the primary parties well, though others also can be involved. For instance, in Section 2, we emphasize the value that academics other than scientists can bring to public engagement with science. Conceiving of public engagement with science as multidirectional involves attending to multiple partners' goals, needs, constraints, and relationships with public constituents. This enables the development of initiatives that benefit from researchers' perspectives as well as the expertise of their community partners and that influence all involved parties in desired ways. Partnership between academic researchers and community organizations can also provide researchers with a route to effectively assessing the needs of and establishing relationships with the targeted public. Further, many forms of public engagement are multidirectional insofar as public participants also influence one another during the engagement.

As we discussed early in this section, the interrelationships between science and the public are extensive and unavoidable. Public engagement with science thus has significance for science no less than it does for society. AAAS (2016) specifies a vision of ultimate goals of public engagement with science that reflects this. Their vision includes, among other items,

1. Sound, evidence-informed public decision-making on science-related issues
2. Dialogue on critical science-society issues embedded in public discourse
3. Research that is responsive to societal needs and interests
4. Resilient STEM workforce
5. Science embedded in daily life

The AAAS vision incorporates not just changes to public life but changes to the enterprise of science as well, and it involves the aims of understanding, identity, trust, access, and interest discussed above. This AAAS list thus offers a way to summarize some of our main points in this introduction to public engagement with science. Let's briefly consider how this list relates to public life and the enterprise of science. The first item regards effective use of scientific expertise for public ends – a public-directed, knowledge-based aim. The second item is also public directed, but about affect, attitudes, and discourse, perhaps indirectly also trust, rather than any specific outcome of knowledge or understanding. The third and fourth items are science-directed, about responsiveness of research to public concern and access and inclusion in the STEM workforce. The fifth item is just about the connection between science and public life itself, suggesting that interconnection between science and the public may sometimes not just be instrumental but a goal in and of itself.

1.5 Goal and Structure of This Element

Public engagement with science is gaining currency as the framing for a variety of outreach activities related to science and as an object of study in its own right. As suggested in our discussion so far, key features of this approach to outreach include recognition of a variety of aims beyond simply increased public understanding and commitment to bidirectional influence. However, knowledge bearing on the topic of public engagement with science is still largely siloed in a variety of disciplines, and public engagement activities often are conducted without support from relevant theory or adequate models of similar activities. This Element will set the stage for the series to follow, *Elements in Public Engagement with Science*, by delineating the target of investigation, establishing the importance of cross-disciplinary[4] collaboration and community partnerships for effective

---

[4] In this Element, we use the term "cross-disciplinary" to refer to communication or projects that involve participants with distinct academic or professional backgrounds. We reserve the term "interdisciplinary" for communication or projects that incorporate perspectives from multiple academic or professional backgrounds. The distinction is subtle and not very important for the purposes of our project.

public engagement with science, examining the role public engagement with science plays and could play in academic institutions, and providing some initial resources to learn more about the theory and practice of public engagement with science. This Element is primarily written for an academic audience interested to get more involved in public engagement, but we hope it is also useful to public engagement practitioners as a window into relevant academic knowledge and cultures. Additionally, the series as a whole is designed to incorporate and respond to practitioners' expertise and concerns as well as academics'.

In this first section, we have identified public engagement with science as a potential target for development of theory and explicit best practices. We defined *public engagement with science* as attempts to intervene on some aspect(s) of how some segment of the public relates to science, to the end of improving the relationship (Section 1.1). Aims may consist in a variety of aspects of understanding, identity, trust, access, and interest (Sections 1.2 and 1.3), and improvements to the relationship can and often should involve changes to both science and public communities or institutions (Section 1.4).

Here is the plan for the remainder of this Element. In Section 2, we characterize the range of academic disciplines with relevance for public engagement with science and the nature of that relevance. Public engagement with science is inherently interdisciplinary. Effective public engagement with science requires not only expertise in scientific content but also skills in effective communication, bridging of social divides and cultivation of trust, inspiring interest during brief encounters, and multiple perspectives on science and its roles in society. Doing this well requires insights from or collaboration among people with expertise in science, education and communication, history and philosophy, and more. Existing resources in these and other academic disciplines can meaningfully inform the goals and techniques employed in public engagement, provide theoretical resources for public engagement with science, and offer models of effective engagement.

In Section 3, we make the case that effective public engagement with science should be collaborative. An ambitious, interdisciplinary vision of public engagement with science requires significant collaboration, not just among academic researchers, but also with community partners like experts at museums and zoos, classroom teachers, afterschool care providers, and more. A wide range of stakeholders have an interest in effective public engagement with science, and it is essential to value the expertise, perspectives, and goals of each of them. Collaboration across academic disciplines and, especially, with community partners improves techniques, expands resources, and increases the possibility for continuity and scaling up efforts. On a more practical side, we also address institutional structures at universities that can support public engagement with science efforts.

Section 4 delves further into the range of specific goals that public engagement with science may have, whether the aim is understanding, identity, trust, access, interest, or something else. This section advocates goal-directed design of public engagement with science initiatives and outlines one possible approach to implementing goal-directed design. In this discussion, we appeal to pedagogical resources in course design and learner-centered curricula, suggesting that these apply to many public engagement with science activities (regardless of whether that engagement has educational aims).

Finally, our concluding Section 5 considers the broad range of outreach activities that qualify as public engagement with science, and then discusses the need for and opportunities for teaching and research into public engagement with science. Instruction in public engagement with science can enrich collegiate and post-collegiate science education, and additional curricular opportunities are needed for this instruction. Further, while a wide range of existing research bears on public engagement with science, it also deserves greater focus as a unified target of theoretical and empirical investigation. This is a need this Element, and the series it initiates, aims to address.

2 Disciplinary Expertise Bearing on Public Engagement with Science

The premise of this Element, as well as of the series it initiates, is that public engagement with science is best pursued as a multidisciplinary initiative. A number of bodies of disciplinary knowledge bear on aspects of public engagement with science, as well as knowledge derived from practitioners' expertise, and public engagement with science pursuits will only benefit from expanded influence by them.

In Section 1, we discussed the variety of potential aims[5] public engagement with science may have – including at least understanding, identity, trust, access, and interest – and the possibility of different types of goals in each of these categories, including interventions targeting changes in the public's attitudes and understanding, as well as changes in scientific research and institutions. And yet, research shows that many scientists persist in prioritizing clear communication of scientific findings, despite the ineffectiveness of this in achieving the intended aim of understanding (Besley et al., 2015; Simis et al., 2016) and despite the value of entirely different aims. Resources for transcending this disconnect between the many aims of public engagement and a simplistic

---

[5] As a reminder, we use "aim" to refer to a broad targeted outcome of engagement, such as understanding, identity, trust, access, or interest. "Goal" refers to more specific targeted outcomes, such as helping a public audience to better understand some specific scientific facts.

deficit-model view can be found in a variety of disciplinary research. Multiple academic disciplines can provide resources to inform public engagement with science goals, techniques, and theory, as well as models of robust bidirectional public engagement.

This section explores the range of disciplines relevant to public engagement with science and briefly characterizes the nature of their relevance. Along the way, we will provide some resources as inroads into disciplinary-based knowledge bearing on public engagement with science. The focus is primarily on academic disciplinary knowledge – though some disciplines, like science education and museum studies, are informed by public engagement practice. Section 3's focus on collaboration involves exploring the expertise offered by public engagement practitioners. We also want to stress that this section's introduction to disciplinary resources will by necessity have some limitations. This is because both authors of this Element are philosophers of science. We have some experience with interdisciplinary collaboration, but we do not have expertise in most of the fields characterized here. We encourage the reader to think of this section as a kind of roadmap that we've developed in our efforts to explore what resources are available for the theory and practice of public engagement with science. We are outsiders to most of these disciplines, and it is our hope that the series that this Element initiates will provide deeper explorations of many of these disciplinary resources for public engagement with science.

2.1 Expertise in Public Engagement Goals and Techniques

Expertise in relevant scientific content may seem to be the only or the most important requirement for conducting public engagement with science, but this is seldom the case. As we emphasize throughout this Element, determining proper goals and effective engagement techniques in light of one's aims is essential for successful public engagement with science. Fortunately, expertise relevant to the goals and techniques of public engagement exists across disciplines related to formal and informal education and the social sciences. Here we introduce the disciplines of science education, science communication, museum studies, and community psychology. We also discuss other social sciences later in this section.

Science Education. Science education is one focus within the academic study of education. Research in this field can involve theoretical or empirical evaluation of the aims and approaches of formal science curricula, K-12 learning standards for science, and teacher credentialing. The focus is largely placed on the natural sciences (biology, chemistry, physics, etc.), which receives more attention in curricula and learning standards than social sciences/social studies (psychology, sociology, political sciences, economics, etc.). Some science education research and teacher resources are based on specific scientific disciplines central to curricula, including physics, chemistry, and biology. Science education can occur in many spaces: formal education in K-12 educational settings, as well as postsecondary education and early childhood education. Most commonly, science education focuses on effective teaching with the aim of scientific understanding; the focus is largely placed on helping students learn scientific facts and methods (though some advocate alternative focuses related to instilling trust; see for instance Rudolph, 2023). Science education can also aim to cultivate an interest in science and instill a sense of STEM identity. In some educational contexts, especially K-12 education, there are national or state educational standards that science teaching must meet. In the US, for example, the national science standards at present are the Next Generation Science Standards (www.nextgenscience.org), which some states opted into or adapted, while other states adopted their own different standards. These educational standards and related publications from government departments of education can be a useful resource for learning what is valued in these educational contexts, as well as what research is being drawn on to support the standards. Thus, science education research, policy, and materials can serve as resources to shape the goals and techniques of at least some varieties of public engagement initiatives.

In addition to formal science education, informal science education consists in designed learning activities in settings outside of a traditional classroom.[6] Given that individuals only spend approximately 5 percent of their lives in formal classroom settings, varieties of informal learning can be key to fostering scientific literacy in society (Falk and Dierking, 2010). Museums, zoos, and libraries, for example, offer members of the public brief encounters with science, but in a context where they are primed for an educational experience. Some informal settings can attract and serve an audience of a variety of ages, from children to adults, each having different engagement needs. There are significant overlaps between literatures on formal science education and informal science education, and informal science education often is also responsive to formal educational standards. Yet informal science education also includes activities pursued with a broader definition of learning, and these varieties of informal science education may offer models of goals and techniques aligned with aims other than increased understanding of science – such as identity, trust,

---

[6] We follow the National Research Council (2009) in using "informal science education" broadly to refer to less structured science learning outside formal educational contexts. Note, however, that some call this "non-formal science education," reserving "informal" for only activities not pursued with learning as a goal.

usefulness, or simply fun. In addition to research on learning, informal education also has a robust practice of evaluation.

Science education research and resources can inform public engagement with science theory and practices in several ways. First, those interested in conducting public engagement can find models and guidance for science learning in formal and informal educational settings. Further, science education research can provide pedagogical principles and resources to guide implementation details of public engagement initiatives, including regarding inclusive teaching practices. This research can also guide how goals and techniques may be tailored to different audiences. Science education has a vast number of academic publications and journals on informal and formal STEM education. (See, for instance, journals like *International Journal of Science Education, International Journal of STEM Education, Journal of Research in Science Teaching, Science Education, Science & Education,* as well as books like *Routledge Handbook of Research on Science Education*.) There is also disciplinary-focused science education research, such as work targeting biology or physics teaching, which can be useful to public engagement targeting topics in these disciplines. Further, colleges and universities offering degrees in teaching often have science education as an available specialty, which can be an avenue to finding collaborators and local expertise bearing on potential public engagement initiatives. There are also extensive science education professional associations and networks, such as the National Center for Science Education (NCSE, https://ncse.ngo), National Informal STEM Education Network (NISE, https://www.nisenet.org) in the US, National Science Teaching Association (NSTA, https://www.nsta.org), and National Association for Research in Science Teaching (NARST, https://narst.org).

Museum Studies. Museum studies is the academic investigation into museum design and use. Main focuses include curation, that is, managing museum collections and designing exhibits; education, that is, developing programming and structures to support visitors' experiences and learning; and management, that is, business administration and public relations. Museum careers tend to divide into these focuses – curators, educators, and management – where the first tend to have relevant subject-matter credentials (e.g. a PhD in paleontology) and the second tend to have training in informal or non-formal education. Curators tend to have roles in collection-based museums. Increasingly, museum studies has also developed research lines critical of traditional museum design, intended audiences, and societal roles. These criticisms have led to attempts to rethink the purpose of museums, as well as how they should relate to local communities and to the cultures of museum artifacts. One important strand in that research is the advocacy of decolonization efforts, or ways to transform museums away from their legacy in colonialism by cultivating more diverse audiences and rethinking the treatment and presentation of artifacts to be more respectful and responsive to the cultures they come from (Lonetree, 2012; Adams, 2017; Onciul, 2015).

Museum spaces and programming are, of course, themselves instances of public engagement with science and are also potential opportunities for partnership in public engagement initiatives by academics and others. It is important to consider the opportunities that both curation and museum education may offer for public engagement with science initiatives. Beyond this, principles and techniques from museum studies may inform other kinds of public engagement with science activities, especially when they are similar in circumstances and goals to museum experiences. Museum studies resources may inform, for example, a temporary exhibit in a public non-museum context or science engagement with children in a day-camp setting. Note that museum studies resources overlap with informal science education and science communication resources. Those interested in learning more about museum contexts might seek out colleges and universities that offer a degree, often an M.A., in Museum Studies. Additionally, this field also has its own publications, guides, and journals (see for example Latham and Simmons, 2014; and https://guides.nyu.edu/museum-studies/books).

Science Communication. Science communication is an area of research within the academic study of communication, a social science, and it is also a much broader community of practitioners and researchers focused on wide-ranging forms of communication about science, often called SciComm (Burns et al., 2003). Research in science communication occurs in the disciplines of communication and journalism, as well as in the "science of science communication," and it overlaps with other disciplines we discuss elsewhere, including museum studies and science and technology studies. Science communication research focuses on the effectiveness of broad communication efforts, as well as methodology of how to assess such effectiveness (for an introduction to this field, see Fischhoff and Scheufele, 2013; Kahan, 2015; Jamieson et al., 2017). Attention is also directed at the spread of misinformation and counteracting it (e.g. van der Linden et al., 2017; Lewandowsky et al., 2020). Much of the research in this space is targeted at specific scientific topics, such as climate change or health; specific contexts, such as national setting; and method of communication, such as campaigns (e.g. Goldberg and Gustafson, 2023). Some broad principles can be gleaned from this more specific research, though, including the importance of trusted messengers, clear messages, as well as emotional engagement with and personal relevance to the audience (Matthew Goldberg, conversation). Beyond this focus on the processes of science communication, communication studies also investigate channels and audiences for science communication.

Science communication research increasingly pursues a public engagement approach and, thus, provides resources especially useful to public engagement (e.g. Jensen and Gerber, 2020). Forms of public engagement with science that fit science communication frameworks especially well include public writing, talks, and other forms of broad messaging. Science popularizers like Bill Nye and Neil deGrasse Tyson also fit into this category. As this suggests, the practice of science communication extends well beyond science communication research. The practice of science communication, or SciComm, is defined by Burns et al. (2003, p.191) as:

> The use of appropriate skills, media, activities, and dialogue to produce one or more of the following personal responses to science (the vowel analogy): **A**wareness, including familiarity with new aspects of science; **E**njoyment or other affective responses, e.g. appreciating science as entertainment or art; **I**nterest, as evidenced by voluntary involvement with science or its communication; **O**pinions, the forming, reforming, or confirming of science-related attitudes; **U**nderstanding of science, its content, processes, and social factors.

This delineation of awareness, enjoyment, interest, opinions, and understanding of science partly overlaps with the aims of public engagement with science we identified in Section 1. This definition in terms of skills, media, activities, or dialogue is quite broad and may well include most varieties of public engagement with science. Note that such SciComm activities can be improved with attention to science communication research into effective science communication and its goals and techniques. Resources include the Global Network for Science Communication (https://www.pcst.network) and the journals *Journal of Science Communication* and *Science Communication*. Some universities offer science communication degrees.

Psychology. Multiple subdisciplines of psychology are relevant to public engagement with science in different ways. Developmental psychology and educational psychology provide theories of learning and identity development that are broadly applied in formal and informal education. The specialization of community psychology aims to develop theory, research, and practice focused on the relationship of individuals to society or social systems that create communities. Research often focuses on kinds of social change, including social justice through research and action, community empowerment and sense of community, as well as civic participation (e.g. Riemer et al., 2020). Common focal topics include issues related to physical and mental health, environment, and promotion of diversity. Those who are interested in conducting public engagement with science with aims related to trust, identity, and access may especially benefit from engagement with this discipline and academic publications (see for example, *American Journal of Community Psychology* and https://scra27.org). Community psychology is also one discipline with established community-based research practices, so the field can also serve as a resource for those who wish to conduct scientific research that includes public participation.

This is, of course, not an exhaustive list of disciplines that can productively influence the goals and techniques of public engagement with science initiatives. Depending on the nature of the intended engagement, resources can also be found in fields like professional and creative writing, journalism, early childhood education, educational psychology, and law and public policy, to name a few.

The disciplines discussed here – especially science education, science communication, and community psychology – can also provide resources for the evaluation of public engagement with science initiatives. Assessment and evaluation are important for any goal-directed activity, as this is how success can be gauged, enabling iterative improvements. Program evaluation also creates the opportunity for academic publication about public engagement efforts and their effectiveness. Some evaluation can be very basic, such as recording the number of participants reached and facilitating simple feedback about what the participants enjoyed and their suggestions for the next iteration. Even this basic evaluation is valuable. More involved assessments or evaluations, such as measuring the participants' changes in attitudes or abilities, should draw from methods and validated instruments in the social sciences. When learning outcomes are defined, educational research and evaluation can provide resources for investigating the extent to which these learning outcomes were achieved. More involved evaluations like these are usually best facilitated by collaborating with researchers or evaluators who have relevant expertise. Even simple tools like concluding surveys can benefit from the input of researchers or evaluators with expertise in survey design.

2.2 Theoretical Resources

Other disciplines are well positioned to provide theoretical resources for public engagement with science. These include, among others, history and philosophy of science, science and technology studies, science policy, and applied ethics. By "theoretical resources," we mean ways of thinking about the relationships between science and the public, the goals of public engagement, the status of academic disciplines, and more that can provide a theoretical basis informing how engagement initiatives are pursued.

History and Philosophy of Science. History of science and philosophy of science, sometimes collectively referred to as HPS, investigate the history of scientific institutions and ideas and the theoretical and methodological features of science, respectively. History of science examines how science has proceeded and changed over time, its relationship to social institutions, and more. Philosophy of science studies how science unfolds, its hidden assumptions, its tools and methods, its range of findings, and its relationship to society. This is all essential work for making sense of science and its relationship to the public. For an introduction to the relevance of philosophy of science in particular, see Potochnik (2024). HPS research might focus on specific episodes in science's history or specific varieties of scientific research, or it might engage more broadly with how science has unfolded or the very nature of scientific investigation.

Philosophy of science has developed extensive theory regarding the nature of science, including scientific practices and the relationship of science to society, which has long been recognized as an important topic in science education, outreach, and communication. The importance of scientific practices and science's role in society are increasingly recognized by a variety of scientific and science education bodies, while state and national teaching standards, including the *Next Generation Science Standards*, have shifted to further emphasize scientific practices (McComas and Nouri, 2016). There is evidence that attending to the nature of science, rather than simply focusing on scientific findings, enriches scientific understanding (Chang, 2011; Garik and Benétreau-Dupin, 2014; Hong and Lin-Siegler, 2012; Janssen and Van Berkel, 2014; Garik et al., 2015) and may contribute to the acceptance of controversial or polarizing scientific findings (Lombrozo et al., 2008; Metz et al., 2018). Contextualization of scientific facts with discussion of relevant scientific methods yields significant gains in attitudes, interest, and other motivational factors (Becker and Park, 2011). Potochnik et al. (2024) provides a broad survey of philosophical perspectives on scientific methods and the relationship between science and society. Additionally, feminist philosophy of science has focused on the role of values, identities, and trust in science and the production of knowledge (Richardson, 2010). Some historians and philosophers of science have authored books about science for broad audiences that have been influential – perhaps most notably in recent history, Thomas Kuhn (1962), who is responsible for the concept of a scientific paradigm. A more recent example is (Strevens, 2020), which develops a characterization of the power of scientific methods as a ruthless focus narrowly on empirical data. As historians of science, Naomi Oreskes and Erik Conway (2011) trace the history of how special interests interfered with research on scientific topics of public concern, such as the dangers of smoking and climate change.

Science and Technology Studies. While history and philosophy of science have theoretical tools useful to public engagement with science, science and technology studies (STS) focuses directly on how science and technology relate to society. STS is an interdisciplinary field drawing most frequently on sociology, history of science, anthropology, and political science. In contrast to philosophy's emphasis on theoretical and methodological aspects of science, STS focuses primarily on social, political, and ethical issues related to scientific institutions and the impacts of science and technology on society and the public. Central to STS is the view that the science is inherently a social activity, so the study of science as an enterprise is best done through an interdisciplinary approach. STS examines impact of historical, social, and cultural contexts of science, its development, and its consequences. The field most commonly investigates these topics through the use of qualitative methods, such as interviews and case studies. STS thus offers theoretical resources for engaging public communities in scientific research and advocacy, as a significant research focus is on how science can more fully and equitably serve public communities (Hess, 1997; Jasanoff et al., 2001; Sismondo, 2010).

Science Policy. Science policy focuses on using scientific knowledge to craft various governmental policies, regulations, and structures, as well as the development of policies, regulations, and structures related to the production of science. Since these various policies impact the public, this can be another domain with resources for public engagement with science. In particular, the science of science policy focuses on studying the ways in which science and governmental agencies engage and developing theory and practice of eliciting policy change based on scientific findings, as well as models of the scientific enterprise more generally (Fealing et al., 2011). This academic research space is highly interdisciplinary and aims to bring together social science, behavioral science, and policy communities (see for example, *The Journal of Science Policy & Governance*). There are also organizations that aim to bring scientists, government officials, and other academics together to collaborate on report development and policy, such as the National Science Policy Network, the Union of Concerned Scientists, and the Consortium for Science, Policy, and Outcomes led by Arizona State University.

Applied Ethics. Applied ethics includes disciplinary and interdisciplinary research on ethical considerations for real-world situations. Types of applied ethics with potential relevance for public engagement with science include bioethics, environmental ethics, AI ethics, and research ethics, among others. Bioethics targets ethical and legal issues in biomedicine and biomedical research, which have obvious relevance for public engagement with health research. Public health ethics is of notable relevance; see for example Bayer and Fairchild (2004) and the journal *Public Health Ethics*. Environmental ethics is closely related to sustainability research, its relationships to public concern, and public engagement with environmental science. The Hastings Center (https://www.thehastingscenter.org) provides a number of timely resources on bioethics, environmental issues, and related issues in science. AI ethics is an area of applied ethics emerging in tandem with artificial intelligence, focused on ways in which AI tools can exacerbate or potentially ameliorate inequalities. Research ethics, in turn, provides moral frameworks governing the conduct of scientific research, which relates closely both to implications of research for the public and the inclusion of the public in scientific research. Iltis and MacKay (2020) is a collection of research ethics work by many authors. Also of potential relevance is political theory; for example, Schroeder (2022) advocates a political rather than ethical approach – that is, engaging with deliberation among people rather than with ethical principles – to navigating relationships between science and the public.

These fields can provide various kinds of theoretical resources for how public concern or priorities may shape scientific research and public engagement with science. Above we have flagged some central books and key concepts from each field for those interested in learning more.

2.3 Engagement Models from Scientific Fields

Scientific disciplines have obvious relevance to the scientific content of public engagement with science initiatives, as we discuss in Section 2.5. But scientific disciplines – both natural and social sciences – also have other kinds of relevance for public engagement with science initiatives. For example, firsthand experience with research activities can contribute to engagement initiatives, as when scientists discuss their experiences or participate in open labs in museums. More broadly, approaches to engagement and education in different scientific disciplines can be used as models to inspire and inform public engagement in other fields.

Engagement in the Natural and Social Sciences. Modes of public engagement in the natural sciences and in the social sciences tend to be very different. In the natural sciences, the focus is often placed on sharing content knowledge or inspiring interest and appreciation of that knowledge. Activities might focus on conducting or recreating classical experiments; showcasing and inviting engagement with plants, animals, or minerals; touring labs; or demonstrating the science behind familiar technologies. In contrast, in the social sciences, public engagement is more often directed at influencing policy and practice with social scientific insights and using community perspectives to motivate and influence research. For example, the Ohio Policy Evaluation Network (OPEN) conducts social-science research on how public policy affects reproductive health and equity in Ohio and nearby states. The stated aim is to "improve reproductive health outcomes and uphold autonomy for all Ohioans" (OPEN website: https://open.osu.edu/about-open/). Each of these focuses – sharing knowledge and inspiring interest, and influencing policy and practice – can be valuable, and sometimes can be pursued in concert. But there tend to be well-explored paths for how specific scientific fields conduct public engagement, so examining public engagement conducted in other disciplines – even very different disciplines from one's own – for different models of engagement can be instructive. Considering modes of public engagement in disciplines distant from one's own can help one recognize the potential for novel modes of engagement.

Disciplinary-Based Educational Research (DBER). Disciplinary-based educational research is "an empirical approach to investigating learning and teaching that is informed by an expert understanding of [STEM] disciplinary knowledge and practice" (NRC, 2012). Where the scholarship of teaching and learning (SoTL) focuses on inquiry into student learning and improving one's own teaching and curriculum in light of pedagogical best practices, DBER focuses on empirical investigation of different educational strategies, assessments, and practices. Though SoTL and DBER exist along the same continuum, DBER is more frequently engaged in by STEM communities due to its reliance on systematic research methods, akin to scientific inquiry (https://soler.columbia.edu/sites/default/files/content/DBER%20Guide%20Figs/SOLER_Faculty Guide_062920.pdf). DBER is thus directly relevant for engagement targeting college students. Students in undergraduate general-education college courses are, after all, the largest segment of the nonspecialist public that most academic researchers engage with directly. Effective approaches to teaching and learning specific to the content and circumstances of scientific disciplines can meaningfully improve this engagement – leading not only to better content knowledge but also other outcomes related to trust, identity, and interest.

DBER findings also have a much broader potential relevance for public engagement with other kinds of audiences. This research commonly aims to identify effective ways to teach specific scientific content or techniques, and this can be relevant to public engagement outside the classroom, especially when the aims include increased understanding. So, while DBER research applies directly to college instruction, this research can also indirectly inspire engagement techniques relevant to outreach in, say, high-school science classes, STEM afterschool clubs, or science experiences targeted at adult learners.

Community-Based and Action Research. Scientific research that includes members of the public as part of the research progress in ways that go beyond merely serving as research subjects goes by several different names, including community-based participatory research (CBPR), action research, community science, and citizen science. These approaches vary in how and why they include public participants. In some cases, the public primarily assist with data collection or analysis, while other research activities are co-created with the participating public, with scientists and members of the public together designing the research questions and coordinating in data collection and analysis. Community-based participatory research and action research in particular offer models for public participation in scientific research that goes beyond data collection to include public participation in all aspects of research design and implementation. This involvement enables community priorities to shape the research questions, approaches to data collection, and utilization of findings.

These practices for involving public participation in scientific research have grown up in a variety of fields, largely in the social sciences, including anthropology, community psychology, educational research, and health research, among other fields (Vaughn and Jacquez, 2020). Inclusion of the public is much broader than just these research traditions, especially in environmental and health research, but rationale and methodology are often less well developed. There is thus an opportunity for public engagement involving participation in scientific research in other fields to gain insights from CBPR and action research traditions, particularly in how to effectively and justly employ participatory techniques and how to more deeply involve public participants in research. Some practical guidance for community-based research is provided by Ross et al. (2010). Including public participation in scientific research, and doing so thoughtfully so as to include targeted communities and adequately incorporate their values and voices (Dunlap et al., 2021), is one important variety of public engagement with science. See Section 5 for more on this form of public engagement.

2.4 Scientific Content

Up to this point, this section on disciplinary resources for public engagement with science has focused almost entirely on resources for public engagement practices rather than scientific content of engagement. One reason for this is the outsized emphasis that scientists interested in public engagement tend to place on content-knowledge, as discussed above (Besley et al., 2015; Simis et al., 2016). Another reason is that public engagement practices generalize quite well across forms of engagement, while content varies significantly. The disciplines that can provide relevant content knowledge accordingly also vary.

Nonetheless, in this last section, we will briefly comment on disciplines that may provide content knowledge for public engagement initiatives. The first obvious place to look for relevant content knowledge are scientific disciplines involved in or targeted with the engagement initiatives. A wide variety of disciplines across the natural and social sciences – as well as engineering, medicine, planning, and more – can be relevant in this way. The relevant content may include cutting-edge research breakthroughs or cumulative state of knowledge about some topic. Although scientists are trained to emphasize the novelty and importance of their own research, broader, more well-established knowledge is often more valuable as the content of public engagement. If the focus is recent research breakthroughs, emphasis usually should not be placed on radical transformation or novelty but continuity and extension of existing knowledge. Such framing supports public trust in science and a recognition of the value of scientific consensus, which are valuable ends, even if it decreases the appearance of novelty (Slater and Scholfield, 2022). Similarly, while research publications must emphasize the novel contribution the publication makes to the state of knowledge, public engagement initiatives often benefit from bringing in much broader content and emphasizing general characterizations and connections rather than highly specific insights.

In keeping with the different aims of understanding, identity, trust, access, and interest we identified in Section 1, notice also that the role played by content knowledge in public engagement may not be to increase public participants' understanding of that content. Perhaps instead the goal is to give access to an insider's perspective to shift identity perception, to provide insight into a research consensus to increase trust, raise new questions the participants hadn't considered, or simply to spark interest through fascination and fun. To further any of these goals, content knowledge need not be transferred to the participating public during engagement.

We also saw in Section 1 that even the aim of understanding may not relate straightforwardly to scientific content. Understanding of scientific methods and practices may be especially valuable (e.g. Weisberg et al., 2021). Accordingly, scientific disciplines are not the only place to turn for content knowledge relevant to public engagement. For example, we described in Section 2.2 how history and philosophy of science can be relevant to public understanding of these topics. Science and technology studies, applied ethics, and more can also provide relevant content knowledge about the practice of science and its relationship to society.

2.5 Conclusion

In this section, we have explored how a range of different academic disciplines can be relevant to public engagement with science. For expertise bearing on the goals and techniques of public engagement with science, one might explore science education, museum studies, science communication, and community psychology. For theoretical resources relevant to public engagement, one might consider history and philosophy of science, science and technology studies, science policy, and applied ethics. One might find models for how public engagement can be carried out by considering different fields in the natural and social sciences, disciplinary-based educational research, and community-based and action research in the social sciences. And, finally, a wide range of science, engineering, medical, and applied fields can influence the content of public engagement with science initiatives. Yet the proper goal of public engagement is often something other than transferring knowledge of scientific content to the participating public. And, scientific consensus positions and established knowledge tend to be more relevant than cutting-edge research breakthroughs.

This discussion has also provided some initial resources as ways to gain disciplinary knowledge relevant to one's public engagement plans or priorities. No one involved in public engagement with science – academic or engagement professional – will engage deeply in all of these disciplines. But a clearer sense for this broad constellation of disciplines and the resources each has to offer can make public engagement efforts more efficient and effective. While the section's focus was primarily on academic disciplinary knowledge, some of the disciplines we surveyed, like science education and museum studies, are informed by public engagement practice. In the following section, we explore how collaboration can be used to incorporate disciplinary expertise as well as the expertise of public engagement practitioners.

3 An Essentially Collaborative Endeavor

In Section 2, we surveyed disciplinary resources that bear on public engagement with science in one way or another. This sets the stage for the point we will develop in this section: activities in public engagement with science benefit from collaboration across disciplines and with a variety of practitioners and organizations. As we've seen, several academic disciplines have content, methods, and practices that can facilitate and enrich public engagement initiatives. Public engagement with science is also benefited by a further form of collaboration, namely, partnership with public engagement practitioners and community organizations. Public engagement practitioners and community organizations offer relationships with different types of public audiences, expertise and programs that can support public engagement collaborations, and – perhaps most crucially – organizational priorities and knowledge of their public constituents that can shape appropriate goals for public engagement initiatives.

In this section, we address issues related to why and how to collaborate across academic disciplines and with practitioners and community organizations. We begin by exploring how collaboration across academic disciplines and with partner community organizations are important for the effectiveness of public engagement with science initiatives (3.1). Central to fostering effective collaborations is attunement to the various and differing values and goals different collaborators might have. Accordingly, this section then turns to resources for managing collaborations between academics and community organizations (3.2). Regarding higher education contexts, we survey institutional structures of colleges and universities that can be leveraged to facilitate and support public engagement (3.3) and how benchmarks of academic success, especially reappointment, promotion, and tenure requirements, can better support public engagement (3.4). This section is most directly relevant to academics who conduct or want to conduct public engagement activities, as this is the perspective the authors bring to this project. But, this section can also be useful to public engagement practitioners who want to motivate or improve their collaborations with academics.

3.1 Collaborating across Academic Disciplines and with Community Partners

In Section 1, we defined public engagement with science as attempts to intervene on some aspect(s) of how the public relates to science, to the end of improving the relationship. This definition immediately suggests reasons why collaboration across academic disciplines and with community organizations may be helpful for public engagement with science initiatives. Effective public engagement with science requires not only expertise in scientific content but also skills like effective communication, bridging of social divides and cultivation of trust, inspiring interest during brief encounters, and multiple perspectives on science and its roles in society, as well as the cultivation of relationships. Doing all of this well requires collaboration among people with a wide variety of expertise.

To start, as we saw in Section 2, a number of different academic disciplines have developed research and skills bearing variously on the goals and techniques of public engagement, theoretical resources for public engagement, evaluation of the effectiveness of public engagement activities, and models of effective public engagement of a variety of kinds. Cross-disciplinary collaboration is thus valuable in making available more of this variety of resources.

Furthermore, interdisciplinary and cross-disciplinary research is strongly encouraged by various science organizations, academies, and grants agencies as a path toward advancing fundamental understanding or a way to solve problems, as often solutions are beyond the scope of one discipline alone (National Academies of Sciences, 2005). The ability to conduct inter- and cross-disciplinary work is also seen as a critical skill to cultivate in graduate STEM education (National Academies of Sciences, 2018).

There is reason to think that adopting an interdisciplinary approach is particularly important to delivering meaningful public engagement with science (and training in public engagement with science) that follows the pattern outlined in this Element. An interdisciplinary approach facilitates the development of expertise not only in scientific content but also in effective communication, bridging social divides, cultivating trust, and inspiring interest during brief encounters (Miller, 2001; Sturgis and Allum, 2004; Harry and Klingner, 2007; Nisbet and Scheufele, 2009; Groffman et al., 2010; de Melo-Martín and Intemann, 2018). These needs are increasingly salient once public engagement looks to aims beyond understanding scientific content and formats beyond the dissemination-based deficit model. Academics with experience in interdisciplinary collaboration are also better able to articulate the meaning and value of interdisciplinarity not just for science but for society as well (Borrego and Newswander, 2010). And yet existing research in effective public engagement with science approaches is scattered across disciplinary specialties, often siloed in distinct literatures on communication, science education, museum education, psychology, digital humanities, professional writing, and others, and existing graduate public outreach training tends to target specific disciplines (e.g. Laursen et al., 2012). For this reason, research on effective facilitation of interdisciplinary work is likely to be another domain to bring to bear on public engagement (Gunawardena et al., 2010; Hubbs et al., 2020; Pfirman and Martin, 2010; Derrick et al., 2011).

Effective intervention on some interface between science and the public thus benefits from a wide variety of academic disciplinary resources and also attention to how to bring to bear resources from different disciplines. But these are not the only needed resources or collaborations. Professionals in a wide variety of community organizations also have expertise, skills, perspectives, and relationships that improve public engagement with science initiatives. Relevant types of professionals include, to start, educators in informal or non-formal science education organizations, such as museums, zoos, and aquariums, as well as in school and childcare settings. Other staff in museums, zoos, etc., such as curators or sustainability staff, can also be relevant to shaping public engagement plans. For other kinds of projects, journalists or other media professionals may be important collaborators. Community leaders, government officials, and nonprofit professionals are another set of public-engagement practitioners who can serve as resources for some kinds of public engagement with science initiatives.

Public engagement professionals can serve as resources and collaborators in a number of ways. For one thing, these professionals have cultivated expertise in public engagement relevant to their professional context – such as science museums, kindergarten classrooms, local media, and regional sustainability initiatives, to give just a few examples. These areas of expertise and skillsets may be drawn from directly in collaborative initiatives or simply can be a source of guidance and feedback. It might be worth considering not only practitioners' expertise but also their distinctive perspectives. Such perspective includes professionals' knowledge of their organization's needs, priorities, resources, and constraints, and it often also includes insight into constituents' interests and concerns, as well as institutional knowledge of what's been done in the past and how it went. Another way in which public-engagement professionals can serve as a resource is through the relationships they have developed. This can include personal rapport with relevant publics, mailing lists, the expectations they've cultivated in those who engage with them, and more.

An ambitious, interdisciplinary vision of public engagement with science requires significant collaboration, not just among academic researchers but also with community partners like experts at museums and zoos, classroom teachers, afterschool care providers, and more. Initiatives benefit from exploring models developed by others, deploying initiatives with sensitivity to contextual factors, and engaging with partners from other disciplines and in professional practice whose collaboration may strengthen the initiative. A wide range of stakeholders have an interest in effective public engagement with science, and it is essential to value and deploy the expertise, perspectives, and goals of each of them.

3.2 Working Effectively with Community Partners

Section 3.1 emphasized the importance of collaboration for effective public engagement with science, but individuals with different expertise and focuses can find it challenging to initiate collaborations. This is perhaps especially acute for collaborations between academics interested in public engagement and public engagement professionals. We thus turn now to a consideration of how academic researchers and public engagement professionals at community partner organizations can work effectively together. The overarching principle of this discussion is that effective collaboration always starts from a consideration of the needs, constraints, and priorities of each partner. Achieving this requires navigating myriad small differences in approach between academic and professional cultures. Here are some general guidelines that may be useful for academic researchers approaching community organizations and professionals employed at them – and for public engagement professionals motivated to navigate academic cultures.

To start, academic institutions and community organizations, especially nonprofit organizations, tend to work on different seasonal timelines. Academic institutions are constrained by the academic year, where availability of students and faculty for structured opportunities like courses is largely limited to the fall and spring, while summer can provide an opportunity for more open-ended engagement – but only with sufficient advance planning. The pace of academic initiatives tends to be very slow by the norms of other professions. The seasonal timelines of community organizations are more variable but no less constraining. For example, the funding and thus activities of many nonprofit organizations may be tied to specific grant cycles. Museums often schedule their exhibits years in advance, and they know to expect a rush of visitors when schools are not in session and few visitors in September. Successful collaboration across academic and community organizations thus requires sensitivity to and accommodation of the timelines and constraints that shape each organization's work. Consider, for example, that the authors have had a conversation with a funding director of a local nonprofit organization who expressed the view that it is very risky to work with academic researchers, given all that is at stake for them in projects staying on track for the future grant applications they will need to write on a set timeline. See Ross et al. (2010) for helpful similar considerations for effective partnership in community-engaged research in particular.

Regarding effective communication, note that telephone communication is very uncommon in academic cultures, while email correspondence dominates. In contrast, telephone communication is more common in many other professions and reliance on email correspondence less common. Trying different modes of communication – telephone, email, and in-person and virtual meetings – can be useful. In many cases, initiating a conversation about communication norms and preferences, including modes of communication, frequency, and speed of response, can be helpful. Meeting to learn more about the other individual or organization and to brainstorm potential collaborations can be especially valuable. One thing to be mindful of is that times of availability may differ – with early mornings and lunchtimes oftentimes easiest for professionals, while many academics tend to schedule meetings from midmorning through early afternoon. It is often simpler to meet somewhere other than the academic institution, as college and university campuses can be hard to navigate and can have difficult logistics, like parking. It can be helpful to explore what meeting locations will be convenient to all parties, without presuming that other parties have flexibility to travel offsite or are familiar with your work location. Virtual meetings can be convenient, though here too norms differ regarding willingness to meet virtually and what meeting platforms are available. It also can be much easier to connect across differences when meeting in person.

Though this might not be readily apparent to some in a university setting, academic researchers are typically perceived as high powered not only by public audiences but also by many professionals with whom we engage. It can be tempting for academic researchers to presume that other professional cultures are similar to academic cultures, and that academic researchers know enough about other kinds of organizations and professions to have new ideas of use to them. But it is worth resisting these and similar assumptions. Instead of centering one's own values and expectations, an academic researcher can get a long way by reaching out to potential partners before their plans are already formed, by asking questions (and listening to the responses!), and by being responsive to others' organizational norms and priorities. Conversely, we have witnessed public engagement professionals adeptly managing collaborations with academics by clearly and directly indicating their opportunities, needs, and limitations, as well as what from the collaboration is of interest and potential value to their organization.

The point about reaching out to potential partners early, before plans are formed, deserves additional emphasis. We authors, as directors of our university's Center for Public Engagement with Science, have seen many examples of academics planning public engagement initiatives and only reaching out to a planned partner when the plans have been formulated, or even reaching out only with a final deliverable. (We will admit that both of us have also done these things!) There's often also an implicit assumption that the plan or deliverable is of value to the community organization. For example, a researcher may intend to produce materials for a museum exhibit related to a research project they are conducting. But, simply passing deliverables on to a community organization is a strategy nearly guaranteed to fail. This approach does not take into account the organization's needs nor their existing plans and need for advanced scheduling, and it precludes the possibility of their expertise and interests shaping the initiative. Staff of the community organization almost certainly have expertise that could have helped to produce a better final output, and some may even feel overlooked or insulted by the failure to consult with them. In a museum, for instance, curators are professionals trained and tasked with creating exhibits, and museum educators have professional training and job responsibilities related to museum programming, whereas academic researchers rarely have either set of skills and insights. (Academics, imagine if someone with no professional background in your discipline called out of the blue to offer you a new syllabus for a course you had developed over the past decade, since they too have interest in that topic.) Too often deliverables generated by academics eager to conduct public engagement, but without the collaboration of community partners, results in materials on a shelf somewhere, gathering dust.

Instead, approaching potential partners early in the planning stages of a project, with openness to their ideas and constraints, enables thoughtful co-creation of initiatives that meet both parties' needs. This maximizes the chance of creating an initiative that is well suited for its context, that meets the community partner's needs and interests, that is aligned with the academic's goals and abilities, and that will have lasting impact. Engaging with partners early is also the best route to successful engagement with the desired public participants, as it enables successful partnership with organization(s) that can maximize the effectiveness of the initiative and gain access to the intended public participants. Many of the points made about effective collaboration in this section also extend to effective engagement with members of the public as well. It pays to be curious about the values and needs about the segment(s) of the public you intend to engage with, rather than anticipating what they will need and what you think they should value.

We will conclude this section with a list of five tips for developing partnerships between academics and professionals at community organizations, some of which relate to discussion above. First, there is no single formula. Instead, every project and community partnership will be context dependent, depending on the needs, priorities, and constraints of academic collaborators, community partners, and public participants. Second, don't reinvent the wheel. Instead, start by exploring what projects, groups, and organizations already exist within your university or nearby universities and the community. Relevant affinity programs, structures, and communities almost certainly already exist, and, by tapping into these, you collaborate rather than compete for audience or participants.

Third, know your partner. Do your "homework" before an initial meeting so you are well prepared with relevant questions. Be curious about their interests and ideas. As the project develops, learn their needs, priorities, and what works well for them, and actively listen to them. Public engagement professionals often have insight into the targeted public participants, so should be heeded in their advice on this as well. Public engagement professionals, be transparent about how collaboration with academics is useful and what would be valuable to your organization. Fourth, find opportunities to co-create. Even as you prepare for an initial meeting, avoid the urge to come prepared with a fully developed idea. Instead, arrive ready to brainstorm collaboratively, with a few ideas and seeking alignment with the other party's goals and interests. And remember to build their input and feedback into your plans. Moving too quickly, without checking in enough, is a real risk.

Fifth and finally, listen and be responsive to your collaborator's goals. Understand, appreciate, and take into consideration the needs, values, and goals of the organization and the community it serves, as well as resources available (and not available) to them. Reflect on and ask about the following: How will this organization benefit from the initiative? What resources will it cost them? Is the initiative meeting a need they have? Consider the possibility that the initiative or your collaboration may be welcome but still a net cost to the organization. You may need to find resources to fund the organization's participation in your initiative. These suggestions are summarized in Table 2.

Collaboration between academics interested to engage with the public and professionals and organizations outside academia increases the effectiveness of most public engagement with science initiatives by bringing to bear a variety of relevant expertise, tailoring initiatives to the local community context, refining plans to meet real needs and to connect effectively with public participants, and ensuring initiatives are goal-oriented and sustainable over time. In this section, we've surveyed recommendations for how to establish effective collaborations. A theme has been variety: there's no single way to collaborate and no list of proper collaborators. Instead, effective partnership for public engagement initiatives is resourceful and open-minded.

3.3 Making Use of Academic Institutional Structures

In the previous section, we considered features of effective academic–practitioner partnerships in public engagement with science. In this section and the next, we turn our attention to how academic institutional structures can be engaged with to support public engagement with science – and then to how those structures might be improved to better support effective public engagement. An extension of the idea that resources for public engagement with science are found in different academic disciplines is the idea of looking to universities' institutional structures for support and insight. The structure and function of university administrative offices vary widely, of course, so the specific details at any given university may well be distinctive. But it's possible to provide some general guidance on what kinds of institutional structures at universities and other academic entities may be relevant and how these might be useful. Note that, while this section and the next are perhaps most relevant to academics pursuing public engagement initiatives, public engagement professionals outside of academic contexts might find this information useful in facilitating their collaborations with academic researchers.

To start, it's worth exploring what initiatives and partnerships already exist at your institution or academic institutions in your region. These might offer

Table 2 Five pieces of advice for developing initiatives with academic and community partners

1. No single formula	Projects depend on the needs, priorities, and constraints of partners and public audiences
2. Don't reinvent the wheel	Explore what groups already exist and how you can collaborate
3. Know your partner(s)	Be prepared with background information and curious about partners' interests and ideas
4. Find opportunities to co-create	Engage in collaborative brainstorming; build input and feedback into your plans
5. Listen and be responsive	Consider the needs, values, goals, and resources of partners and relevant communities

opportunities for collaboration, a model of successful initiatives, or simply relationships through which you can learn about and be connected to potential partners within or outside the university. The list of disciplines in Section 2 can be used to guide a search of a university's website for potentially relevant faculty. Invite conversation to learn about their efforts and, if the conversation is fruitful, to explore the possibility of collaboration. One potential difficulty is that public engagement activities can be hard to identify in traditional representations of academic activities, as on websites or curriculum vitae. It can take time and patient exploration to get a full picture of relevant activities and potential collaborators at an academic institution. Sometimes cross-disciplinary collaborations can provide useful connections to public engagement professionals who might be potential collaborators or even entry points to accessing relevant public audiences, such as a well-established public discussion series held in partnership with a local organization with a loyal audience.

A variety of different university administrative offices can focus on community engagement, and these can also serve as resources and connection points between academic researchers and students and community partners or public audiences. Some universities and colleges or smaller administrative units within them have offices of community partnership. Diversity, equity, and inclusion (DEI) offices sometimes focus on community engagement as well. In the authors' experience, community engagement offices may focus largely or entirely on undergraduate volunteer engagement and not be prepared to support the public engagement efforts of faculty or connect public engagement practitioners to faculty. Nonetheless, these offices may have established deep relationships between the college or university and relevant community organizations that can be redeployed in new ways. Community engagement offices can also be a way to get students, especially undergraduate students, involved in public engagement efforts spearheaded by community organizations or faculty, perhaps through a service-learning course or paid or volunteer internships. Some office on campus is almost certainly focused on university–community relations. This might be the same community engagement or DEI office, or it might be distinct. These offices too are usually not well positioned to facilitate faculty public engagement efforts, but they may be able to provide information about existing and past outreach at the institution, resources on campus, and perhaps connections to relevant community organizations.

Another resource for faculty to consider is their college or university's grants office. Grant officers often know who at the institution is doing similar work from reviewing faculty grant proposals. Similarly, if one's university has one or more offices that award internal grants, they may also have a sense of faculty with complementary interests or activities, and they may be willing to help "matchmake," putting you in touch with these researchers. Some universities also have a broader-impacts or research- and knowledge-mobilization officer or office – that is, an office specifically dedicated to helping researchers connect with the community for the purposes of enhancing the competitiveness of grant proposals. If such an office exists at your institution or an academic institution you want to connect with, it can be very helpful in connecting you to researchers with relevant interests and activities or to potential off-campus collaborators. Of course, different kinds of offices exist at different institutions, and every office is run differently. Many times, just as with seeking potential collaborators, it takes many conversations of open brainstorming to find individuals with ideas and aims aligned with your own.

Another potential resource at academic institutions for public engagement initiatives is the institution's alumni office or foundation. The alumni of an institution are members of the public, and alumni offices typically arrange programming and other opportunities for alumni. The alumni office thus may be looking for public speakers, researchers to feature in alumni events or in an alumni newsletter or magazine, and so on. Of course, public engagement activities with the alumni office reach a particular segment of the public: university-educated adults, usually in the region of the institution. This is only suitable for certain kinds of public engagement with science initiatives, but it can be a great opportunity when it is suitable. The targeted demographic of alumni events also can have some advantages. This is an audience of mature adults who are primed, given the university-focus, to engage in a learning experience. Alumni offices can also offer public engagement professionals, especially those who happen to be alumni of the institution, avenues in to connecting with and influencing the outreach activities of the institution, its faculty, and its students.

Beyond offices and people at academic institutions, it's also worth considering potential alignment with the university's strategic vision or institutional priorities. Even if there is no office with this as its mission, societal and community impact of research and teaching activities is often recognized as a central goal by colleges and universities – even if these institutions are not effectively aligned behind this goal. Thus, considering how your public engagement with science priorities align with institutional priorities can be a route to finding institutional connections, institutional attention, and perhaps institutional investment. Effective collaborations between parties at an academic institution and community organizations can be a ready way to signal community impact to the institution. It can also be worth considering how your intended public engagement with science activities align – or may be reworked to align – with diversity, equity, and inclusion priorities of the academic institution. Oftentimes DEI efforts are seen as related to community relations and partnership, which makes public engagement initiatives potentially relevant. And, just as alignment with alumni office priorities leads to the prioritization of a certain segment of the public, alignment with institutional DEI efforts can lead to a prioritization of accessing underserved communities, especially locally, which can lead to impactful engagement.

College and university courses can also offer opportunities for some public engagement with science initiatives. For academics interested in public engagement, one particularly relevant segment of the public is the students in our classrooms. Certain kinds of courses or individual class meetings can provide opportunities for public engagement activities with goals related to these students' understanding, trust, and connection to science. Undergraduate or graduate courses can also provide the opportunity to teach students public-engagement skills or to provide them opportunities to practice public engagement of one kind or another. For example, a course with a focus on environment or sustainability might include a meeting on climate-change advocacy or climate-change communication. Or, a course on community psychology might involve community-engaged research and culminate in a presentation to City Council of the findings (see, for example, https://ucengagingscience.org/2019/12/05/trotts-community-research-senior-capstone-students-present-at-city-hall/). Service-learning courses can involve cultivating community relationships or partners for students to work with in their own, facilitated public engagement. Of course, many of these same courses are opportunities for community organizations and public engagement professionals to connect with students to teach them about public engagement or to partner with classes or a group of students within a class on public engagement initiatives. Collaborations and connections between college classes and community organizations can also be a valuable opportunity for career education (and, for the organizations, for professional recruitment).

Other academic institutions besides colleges and universities can also provide support and models for public engagement with science. Professional societies are a prime example. National and international professional societies, such as the American Chemical Society, the European Geosciences Union, and the International Communication Association, often have missions that include public outreach about their focal discipline and stewardship of that discipline. Depending on the size and existing programming of a professional society, the society's executive office, academic conferences it hosts, or chapters at individual colleges and universities may be interested to support or collaborate in public engagement initiatives relevant to their organization's focal discipline. Professional societies or their chapters can also provide an opportunity for teaching about public engagement. Affinity organizations similarly can be an institutional connection for public engagement initiatives. Affinity organizations at universities or in academic disciplines support members of one or more historically marginalized groups in their involvement in a discipline or profession. Examples include Women in STEM (WiSTEM); Society of STEM Women of Color; the Society for the Advancement of Chicanos/Hispanics and Native Americans in Science (SACNAS); and the National Organization for the Professional Advancement of Black Chemists and Chemical Engineers (NOBCChE). As with professional societies, community outreach and engagement is often a central component of affinity organizations' mission. These organizations thus are potential collaborators for academics conducting public engagement and public engagement professionals alike.

Public engagement with science initiatives can also gain structural support through various research funding mechanisms. For example, all grant proposals to the U.S. National Science Foundation (NSF) are required to include an explicit statement of the potential broader impacts of the research project. Canada and Europe similarly emphasize "research and knowledge mobilization." These requirements are included as a way of representing the importance of societal impact and applications to industry, society, and education. The NSF, for example, states that its Broader Impacts Criterion "may be accomplished through the research itself, through activities that are directly related to specific research projects, or through activities that are directly supported by, but are complementary to, the project" (National Science Foundation, 2015). Grant-funded research is thus a primary opportunity to support meaningful public engagement initiatives.

Yet, while broader impacts or research/knowledge mobilization are a central emphasis of many funding agencies, the reality can fall short of the vision. Many principal investigators consider the NSF's broader impacts criterion to be neither transparent nor practical (Bornmann, 2013), and this criterion is often met with "considerable confusion and dread" (Lok, 2010). Some researchers don't know how to properly address these criteria for societal impact, while others have no interest in societal impact and do not see it as part of their responsibility to conduct this work (Bozeman and Boardman, 2009; Alpert, 2009; Schienke et al., 2009; Frodeman and Holbrook, 2011).

This need for grants to address societal impact is a prime opportunity for collaboration on public engagement with science initiatives. Public engagement professionals and academics knowledgeable about and motivated to conduct public engagement with science may find financial and other support for their engagement initiatives via incorporation into a grant proposal with an aligned research focus. Some grant programs are also geared to support public engagement with science, including by or in collaboration with community organizations, such as the NSF Advancing Informal STEM Learning (AISL) program. Further, public engagement professionals and community organizations can be valuable resources and potential partners for grant-seekers in need of demonstrable societal impacts for their projects. In some cases, community organizations focused on public engagement may be able to standardize broader impacts opportunities related to their outreach or outreach training, enabling these opportunities to be "plug and play" for grant applications from different researchers at colleges and universities in the area. This can be a way to generate consistent public engagement activities – and consistent funding for those activities.

Grants at the state and regional scale, such as through foundations and governmental and educational organizations, are also potential funders of public engagement with science initiatives. Throughout, this Element emphasizes the value of developing public engagement with science initiatives that are localized, embedded in a local context, with local or regional audiences and collaborating organizations. There's a tendency for academics to think about public engagement on the model of research activities: broad dissemination, aimed at national or international venues, equally available to all. But, unlike much traditional academic research, many forms of public engagement with science benefit from personal connections and localization – and, as we saw in Section 1, from bidirectional exchange rather than simply dissemination. These features can make these activities good targets for state or regional, or even municipal, funding.

3.4 Securing Academic Reward for Public Engagement

In the last section, we surveyed academic institutional structures that can support public engagement with science initiatives spearheaded by or involving academics or college students. One major challenge for many academics and graduate students interested in public engagement with science is that academic reward systems as currently structured do not typically value this work. In this section, we turn to look at how academics can navigate those systems – especially reappointment, promotion, and tenure – with an eye to making their public engagement activities count toward professional advancement. We also consider how divisions and institutions can make changes to better support public engagement activities. Though this section's discussion is only indirectly related to collaboration, it builds on the previous section's examination of academic institutional structures, and the topic is of key importance for academics wishing to take on public engagement activities. This discussion might also be useful context for people not working in the academy, including public engagement professionals, to get a better sense for reward structures and requirements faced by academic researchers with whom they collaborate.

The main strategy we advocate for individual academic researchers navigating reappointment, promotion, and tenure processes (colloquially, RPT) is to think strategically about how your public engagement activities might fit into the customary RPT categories of research, teaching, and service. Many public engagement with science activities will count as service to the community, and some may qualify as teaching activities. A challenge is that many institutions place more weight on research contributions than teaching and service contributions – in some cases, significantly higher weight. Community-engaged research is one form of public engagement with science that qualifies as research, but even then, research in partnership with communities can be slower to conduct and less predictable in its outcomes, which can disadvantage community-engaged researchers.

That said, a few adjustments or additions to public engagement activities may help those activities carry more weight for RPT. First, one step is simply to ensure you maximize the visibility and record of success for public engagement activities that qualify as service. For example, you might ensure department and university leaders are aware of your activities, perhaps even witnessing them; record total number of participants and other metrics of successful outreach; and write up the activities or outcomes in some format, like a post on a professional blog or discussion forum, to increase their salience. Second, considering ways to get students involved in your initiatives – in a traditional course as students, as interns, or through other means – can result in those initiatives counting as innovative teaching and mentorship, beyond simply public-facing service. This alignment can also create resources via alignment of public engagement activities with teaching duties and training students to support the initiative. From the perspective of the student, these can be experiences or activities that are important to their education and valuable to list on their CVs or job resumes.

Third, you might also consider whether your public engagement with science activities can support more traditional research accomplishments. Grant support for public engagement initiatives is broadly recognized as a research accomplishment, especially for principal investigators and co-principal investigators of the grant. One might seek grants that support public engagement as the main or one of the main aims, or, as discussed in Section 3.2, one might seek to partner with researchers to support the societal impact of their research. Community-engaged research can support research publications much like traditional research. Other public engagement might be an opportunity for disciplinary-based educational research about the public engagement as a teaching tool, an opportunity for research into the effectiveness of the engagement at accomplishing its goals, or theoretical work on your public engagement initiative as a model, for example. This Element is an example of this approach, as the coauthors are initiating an edited series and authoring an Element in that series to summarize our learning about public engagement with science approaches and opportunities. Cross-disciplinary collaboration can be useful for reconceptualizing public engagement initiatives as research-supporting, as this enables researchers with different skills and disciplinary involvement to engage in ways that may create or enrich research potential. For faculty who participate in graduate degree programs, public engagement initiatives can also support student publications or coauthored publications and dissertations. A similar point holds for undergraduate student coauthorship and theses at undergraduate-student-focused universities.

If you are an academic in a department with control over the documents governing RPT criteria, then you can advocate for public engagement to be included in those categories. Here too, it is worth considering how public engagement might feature not just in service, but in teaching (such as by including an emphasis on service-learning courses and student training or research experiences) and research (such as by including public writing or community-based research as research outputs) as well. Indicating alignment with institutional priorities can be helpful in making the case for such changes, as is finding models in RPT documents in other institutions or other departments of your institution. It can also be helpful to include in RPT or workload documents resources for supporting the RPT cases of publicly engaged faculty, such as statements recognizing how community-based research takes longer than traditional research or discussions of how public engagement enriches research. RPT revisions like moving away from simple quantitative metrics toward contextual evaluation can also be helpful. Public-centered, collaborative public engagement requires thoughtful partnership and the cultivation of trust – neither of which is quick or simple.

Another important consideration is for public engagement to be supported and rewarded for students and faculty at all career stages. Sometimes faculty have the instinct that public engagement activities should be saved for after tenure, after more traditionally appreciated work has been conducted. But this orientation overlooks the depth of early-career faculty interest in public engagement and the sense that some early-career researchers have that public engagement is essential to their academic life (e.g. Fracchiolla, 2023). Supporting early-career researchers – graduate students, postdocs, and pre-tenure faculty – with interests in public engagement may be an excellent way to recruit and retain excellent scholars. To this end, colleges and universities, as well as professional societies, might also find ways to reward these early-career scholars through fellowships or awards. Likewise with funding bodies: for example, the Whiting Foundation Public Engagement Fellowships are aimed toward celebrating and supporting faculty in the humanities who embrace public engagement as part of the scholarly vocation. The American Association for the Advancement of Science also has an Early Career Award for Public Engagement with Science, as well as various fellowships and ambassador programs to support and celebrate scholars who see this work as central to their career. More such awards and fellowships by disciplinary and professional associations can help pave way for the recognition of this work as highly valuable, on par with traditional research or teaching.

So far, this section has focused primarily on how academics who conduct public engagement with science might navigate and find reward for their work within existing academic structures. There is also a need to rethink and re-envision structures and evaluation practices themselves. We noted in the previous section that many institutional priorities and strategic visions include reference to public engagement or community involvement. Nonetheless, there is a need for colleges and universities to reconsider where these activities fit in their priorities as well as how faculty undertaking such work will be supported.

For instance, faculty might be hired in part due to their interest in conducting publicly engaged work or because they are expected to help achieve departmental-, college-, or presidential-level priorities for public engagement. Yet there may not be clear expectations or alignment with the faculty member's official responsibilities as reflected in hiring documents, annual reviews, or applicable RPT criteria. Without alignment between public engagement interests and official responsibilities, faculty who are hired for their strength in community-engaged work may feel they must limit or cease this work in order to find career success. Workload guidelines and promotion criteria thus should reflect the intersection of the institution's values and what the scholar themself deems important in their work (Agate et al., 2022). This will in turn impact what is viewed as appropriate metrics and evidence of productivity. Public engagement success often cannot be measured in the same way as traditional academic activities and is not easily comparable to academic research publications. Likewise, the work may proceed slowly, especially in its early stages, such that when administrative productivity reports and annual reviews emphasize concrete deliverables, like papers or events, and quantity over quality, it can feel as though one must decide between having numerous outputs versus quality outputs aligned with one's professional aspirations. Publicly engaged work needs to "count" not just as a step toward traditional academic goals but as valuable academic work regardless of the kinds of scholarly objects they produce (Agate et al., 2022).

The Charting Pathways of Intellectual Leadership (CPIL) initiative in the College of Arts & Letters at Michigan State University is an example of what such value-aligned institutional practices and change could look like (Fritzsche et al., 2022; see also https://youtu.be/IPFHBJe3QLg). To address the tensions we have noted with what is considered valuable university work and the traditional research-teaching-service classification triad, the CPIL framework asks faculty and staff to report how they shared knowledge, expanded opportunities, and engaged in mentoring and stewardship activities. This framework for intellectual leadership is aligned with traditional RPT criteria (books, articles, and grants) but also allows for the articulation of new criteria, including publicly oriented scholarship and community-engaged and nonprofit work. See Figure 1 for an illustration of the CPIL framework. MSU's College of Arts & Letters has also worked with each unit to apply this framework to their governing document.

In addition to rethinking how university structures facilitate and reward public engagement work in the context of job guidelines and promotion criteria, there is also a need to rethink how to best support academic participation in such work through institutional opportunities and professional societies. As an example of the latter, the American Association for the Advancement of Science (AAAS)'s Center for Public Engagement with Science and Technology may be a model other scientific intuitions can replicate for supporting scientists engaging with the public. Similar to MSU's Charting Pathways in Institutional Leadership initiative, the AAAS Center for Public Engagement with Science and Technology offers a holistic approach, beginning with training and incorporating resources, opportunities to practice engagement, and rewards and incentives for doing public engagement (Kimbrell et al., 2022).

Finally, consider how college and university institutional opportunities may better support public engagement. Just as universities often support faculty teaching development via centers for teaching and learning and support faculty research through offices of research, it may be beneficial to consider

Public Engagement with Science   49

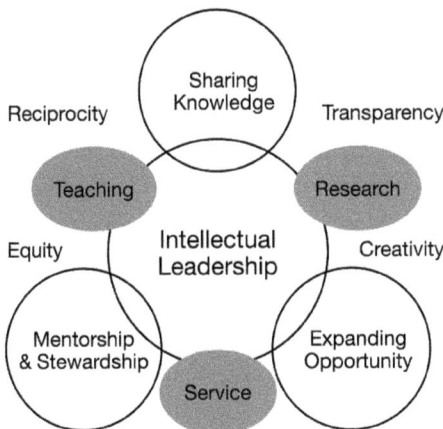

Figure 1 Values, Activities, and Outcomes of Intellectual Leadership, redrawn based on Fritzsche et al. (2022). The outlined, transparent circles represent the ends toward which higher-education activities are directed, that is, the things that should be measured and rewarded. The solid ovals are activities by which those in higher education customarily pursue these ends. An important implication of this framing is that these activities – teaching, research, and service – are not themselves ends. This broadens the recognized possibilities for how higher education pursues its ends. For example, on this model, any form of sharing knowledge is a better measure of success that simply measuring published scholarship. Reprinted by permission of Informa UK Limited, trading as Taylor & Francis Group, www.tandfonline.com.

developing centers for public engagement, whether focused on science or a broader target. Such centers could operate on a variety of models and serve different roles. One model is a university-wide resource office offering support and training programming for faculty and students; hosting public engagement events for the university and community; as well as providing funding awards to support the public engagement activities of faculty, students, staff, and their community partners. Such a resource office might also facilitate connections between university constituents and potential community partners. This kind of office may also be well positioned to consult on broader impacts for faculty grants. Traditional academic departments or newly developed departments might also support public engagement with outreach committees, developing undergraduate and graduate coursework related to public engagement, and other initiatives aligned with research, teaching, and service obligations.

4 Goals and Goal-Directed Design

In Section 1, we discussed how public engagement with science initiatives may have a variety of different aims, including (at least) increased understanding of science, sense of identity, increased trust in science, increased access to participation in science, application of scientific knowledge, and fostering interest in science. These different aims in turn lead to initiatives with different features. In this section we further explore this topic, considering in more depth the various goals of public engagement with science within each of these broad aims and how to design initiatives to address the specific goals at hand. This section also considers how the pedagogical developments of integrated course design and student-centered teaching can be used to influence the design of public engagement with science initiatives.

In Section 4.1, we identify how a move away from a teacher-centered conception of learning toward a student-centered conception parallels the rejection of a deficit-model approach to public engagement with science. We then suggest how a public-centered conception of public engagement with science can be developed, with parallels to a student-centered conception of education. In Section 4.2, we introduce the pedagogical approach of integrated course design as the basis for an approach to goal-directed design of public engagement with science initiatives. Finally, in 4.3, we consider how goal-directed design influences the format of public engagement with science, including relationships with the targeted public, modes of engagement, and roles of community partners.

4.1 Student-Centered Education and the Goals of Public Engagement

The scholarship of teaching and learning (SoTL) focuses on inquiry into student learning and improving one's teaching and curriculum design in light of pedagogical best practices. One theme in the SoTL literature, especially in Western postsecondary education, has focused on a shift in education from a teaching-centered conception of learning toward a student-centered conception of learning (see, for example, Barr and Tagg, 1995; Campbell and Smith, 1997, pp.275–276; Fink, 2013, pp.20–22).[7]

On the teacher-centered conception of learning, knowledge is considered something that experts have that needs to be transferred to the students. Students

---

[7] Here we will refer to the two paradigms as "teacher-centered" and "student-centered." These are sometimes also called, respectively, "teaching-centered" or "content-centered", and "learner-centered" or "learning-centered." This terminology allows us to showcase what we will call "public-centered" public engagement with science.

are considered as relatively passive in their learning, awaiting knowledge and information to be given to them. The role of the instructor, then, is seen as effectively transferring this knowledge from themselves to their students. The primary mode of learning in this paradigm is the memorization of facts and information. This in turn suggests that measures of successful learning relate to how much knowledge a student has gained and their ability to recall this knowledge as needed.

In contrast, on the student-centered conception of learning, the role of the instructor is to help facilitate the construction of knowledge by and with the students. Emphasis is placed not on ensuring students understand a stipulated body of knowledge but rather on identifying where students are in their learning and meeting them there. Students are encouraged not to simply memorize facts but, rather, to understand and to relate knowledge to their experiences and pre-existing ideas. Emphasis is placed on connecting the knowledge more concretely to the world through problem solving, communication, and collaboration. There has been a shift in education away from the teacher-centered conception of learning toward student-centered conceptions of learning, largely because the methods and strategies are more effective across a host of assessments including depth of understanding, short- and long-term knowledge retention, and students' ability to apply knowledge to new contexts.

In some respects, this pedagogical shift from teacher-centered to student-centered learning parallels a shift in public engagement with science away from the deficit model. Recall from Section 1 that the deficit model of public understanding of science is the assumption that the public has a knowledge deficit that experts can simply fill by providing additional scientific information. This deficit model has clear similarities to the teacher-centered conception of learning. We have also seen above that the deficit model has fallen out of favor as a model of public engagement with science. Scientists cannot simply communicate more scientific facts to the public to improve public understanding of scientific issues. This recognition parallels higher education's shift away from a teacher-centered conception of learning toward a student-centered conception.

Because of this parallel, the student-centered conception of learning can be used to inspire ideas about what might replace the deficit model: we might call this a "public-centered" model of public engagement with science.[8] We have surveyed how teacher- and student-centered conceptions of education differ

---

[8] Of course, the parallel between education and public engagement is imperfect, so there will surely be differences between student-centered learning and public-centered engagement. For one thing, we emphasized in Section 1 that not all public engagement aims to produce learning. Still, we think the pedagogical shift to student-centered learning can serve as helpful inspiration for approaches to public engagement with science that move beyond a deficit-model approach.

with respect to conception of knowledge and ways of learning. These different conceptions also impact how students conceptualize their own growth as a learner, how students conceptualize learning goals, the relationship between the student and the instructor, students' and instructors' relationships to the learning environment, the role of power, and ways of knowing. Each of these impacts has potential application to public engagement with science.

McCombs and Whisler (1997, p.10) outline five guiding principles for a student-centered model of learning that we think can be fruitfully applied to public engagement with science.[9] These principles are the following. First, learning opportunities must take into account that learners are distinct and unique. Second, learners' differences include their emotional states of mind, learning rates, learning styles, stages of development, abilities, talents, feelings of efficacy, and other academic and nonacademic attributes and needs. Third, learning is a constructive process that occurs best when what is being learned is relevant and meaningful to the learner, as well as when the learner is actively engaged in creating their own knowledge and understanding by connecting what is being learned with prior knowledge and experience. Fourth, learning occurs best in a positive environment, with positive interpersonal relationships, comfort and order, and in which the learner feels appreciated, acknowledged, respected, and validated. Fifth and finally, learning is a fundamentally natural process; learners are naturally curious and basically interested in learning about and mastering their world.

Applying McCombs and Whisler's (1997) guiding principles in the context of public engagement with science can contribute significantly to the development of a public-centered model of engagement. The first two principles encourage attending to the specific features of public participants, including a wide range of attributes, and anticipating that those features will vary across individuals. The third principle motivates an emphasis on connecting scientific content to public participants' prior knowledge and experience. The fourth principle encourages attention to the circumstances of engagement, including how participants relate to each other and to leaders of the engagement, while the fifth principle encourages a positive view of public participants' interests and abilities.

Another idea from the SoTL literature that can contribute to a public-centered model of engagement is the rejection of the presumption that a teacher is the sole person with relevant expertise, instead acknowledging that students bring expertise as well (e.g. Freire, 1970; hooks, 1994, 2003). This accords with Section 1's discussion of the bidirectional (or multidirectional) influence involved in public

---

[9] Though McCombs and Whisler refer to these as "premises," we think "guiding principles" more accurately captures their role.

engagement with science. And so, a public-centered model of engagement acknowledges that all parties involved – including public participants – have expertise, ideas, and values that should shape the learning experience. A hierarchy still exists in a classroom, insofar as the teacher is still the established expert in the primary topic and assigns grades to students. Similarly, those conducting public engagement with science are expert in the relevant scientific content. But this is not the only expertise relevant to the exchange. All parties in a science engagement experience bring relevant expertise to the table, even if it is very different from researchers' expertise. In some cases, this expertise may be irrelevant or even counterproductive to the goals of the researchers conducting the public engagement, but they are no less relevant to the exchange.

This relates closely to one of the hallmarks of student-centered learning, namely, the decentralization of power away from the instructor. On the teacher-centered model, the instructor is taken to have authority over the educational experience. They are the bearers of information; they are placed at the front of the room; they disseminate the knowledge. In contrast to this, student-centered learning acknowledges that all students possess agency in a learning experience and deserve to be afforded some power over that experience. For example, Paulo Friere advocates for teachers to be partners of students who are pursuing agency, as opposed to enforcers, disciplinarians, and police officers (Friere, 1970; Gutstein, 2007). In disciplines like science in which learning facts is focal, teachers may retain power over this expertise, but there are still opportunities for teachers to share authority with their students in other ways, such as enabling students to make instructional decisions that the teacher then supports and enacts (Basu and Barton, 2010; Keiler, 2018) and being responsive to students' questions and concerns throughout.

Together, these resources inspired by SoTL research motivate six strategies that we suggest as central to a public-centered model of public engagement with science. These strategies are summarized in Table 3. Strategies 1 and 2 of the public-centered model of science engagement relate to the re-examination of the relationship between scientists and public. Strategies 3 and 4 relate to the psychology of learning and engagement processes – taking seriously the lived experiences of the public as fundamental to the conceptualization of how they might engage with science – and how this should inform scaffolded learning or engagement processes. Strategies 5 and 6 relate to how to think about structuring science engagement so that participants actively shape the experience. We say more below about all six strategies.

The first strategy is rethinking power structures. This involves questioning the traditional power structure of expert scientist teaching nonexpert outsiders about science. It can also involve shifting attitudes regarding what counts as scientific

Table 3 Six strategies central to a public-centered model of engagement

Strategy	Description
1. Rethink power structures	Question the traditional power structure of expert scientist teaching nonexpert outsiders; value participant expertise and empower them to shape their experience.
2. Value the public	Take into account key features of participants as a group, as well as variation among individuals, and value what they bring to the table.
3. Engage with participants' belief-value system	Activities should support changes to one part of individual participants' structures of beliefs and values, respecting these structures by minimizing extent of requested changes.
4. Recognize stages of learning	Craft science engagement goals that match expected features of participants, including their structures of beliefs and values.
5. Incorporate metacognition	Promote metacognitive awareness and leverage participants' motivations so they become active participants in the engagement experience.
6. Utilize connections	Encourage participants to see one another and themselves as resources and supports for the renovation in which they are engaging.

expertise. One need not be an academic agricultural scientist to have expertise relevant to agricultural science engagement; a farmer, for example, almost certainly has relevant expertise on topics such as weather patterns, crop rotations, and applicable costs. Especially in order to build social trust, the power structures implicit between expert and presumed nonexpert audience need to be addressed to better recognize relevant expertise of the participating public and to facilitate participants' guidance of how engagement unfolds. Attention to shifting power to public participants can influence the design of interactions. For instance, a "sage on the stage" approach that keeps the scientist or science communicator at the center of the exchange may be replaced with a "guide on the side" approach, challenging participants to direct their own learning rather than just learning what the expert has to say. Just as student-centered learning sets students up to discover facts for themselves, public-centered engagement should facilitate participant leadership over their own experiences. In the end, this can lead to richer and more meaningful engagement.

The second strategy is valuing the public participants. This involves taking into account key features of the audience, participants, or interlocutor as a group, as well as variation among individuals, and valuing what they bring to the table collectively and as individuals. One feature of this is placing trust in participants' epistemic agency, that is, seeing the public participants as having the capacities and opportunities to shape and contribute to knowledge (Miller et al., 2018; Zhang et al., 2022). Beyond this, valuing the public participants involves tailoring the engagement to their needs and interests and anticipating and accommodating variation in the needs and interests of individuals. For example, in community-based research, public participants who are embedded in the community can bring a dramatically different focus and knowledge base than academic researchers who only conduct site visits to the community. Valuing that perspective and enabling it to influence the research is required to make full use of their participation.

The third strategy is engaging with participants' belief-value systems. This is an extension of the idea that public engagement with science initiatives can have goals other than increasing knowledge or understanding. Public participants bring to an engagement experience not just different degrees of knowledge about science but also different identities, values, priorities, and more. Public-centered engagement should form goals and design activities with an eye to participants' systems of beliefs and values – not just their mastery of scientific knowledge. Goals and activities should be designed mindfully regarding what parts of participants' structures of beliefs and values they engage with, and they should respect participants' belief-value structures by minimizing extent of requested changes. People come to the learning process with prior beliefs and experiences that play a role in the construction of knowledge. Public-centered engagement must recognize the fact that we cannot step outside of our current set of beliefs to construct new ones. Neurath (e.g. 1959) famously developed a boat metaphor for generating new knowledge. When a sailor attempts to reconstruct or rebuild the boat while out at sea, the sailor cannot leave the boat and construct from the outside, so enough of the boat must always remain to keep the sailor above water (Cat, 2023). In just the same way, new knowledge must fit with existing beliefs in order to be accepted. Public-centered engagement meets the public participants where they are, considers existing knowledge and values, and considers where they may be ready to go.

Imagine someone who thinks that climate change is a hoax. If that person were to visit a science museum containing an exhibit on climate change, they would not be doing so from an objective point of view. Instead, this hypothetical museum-goer will see the exhibit through a lens informed by the set of beliefs they have at the outset. Perhaps they will assess the content for inconsistencies or look for specific details that they take to be discredited. In fact, *no one* is able to approach a learning environment from an objective point of view disconnected from their prior set of beliefs and values. We can only learn new things from within our current set of beliefs and values. It is thus important to respect the people that we are engaging with, including their current sets of beliefs and values, and to minimize the extent of requested changes. It is not appropriate to expect this museum-goer to suddenly change their understanding of climate change in one visit, as their views on climate change are likely deeply intertwined with a worldview and values they hold. But perhaps they can come away impressed by the depth of the presentation and the extent of the relevant information provided. Perhaps the exhibit can even provide resources to support rethinking how climate science can relate to political or religious identity, thus creating space for a realignment in this museum-goer's beliefs and values. (See Armstrong et al., 2018, for guidance on public engagement about climate change.)

The fourth strategy for public-centered engagement is recognizing that learning occurs in stages. This means that learning is not an all-at-once process; it occurs incrementally, one step at a time, and learning must be scaffolded. The best goals for engagement may well be more modest than outcomes like knowledge mastery or complete trust of scientific findings. Goals may only be one step in a long path toward some ultimate goal regarding participant ability, belief, or value. Perhaps the climate-denying museum-goer cannot be expected to totally change her mind and accept that humans contribute to climate change in one museum visit. This might be too much of a departure from her current set of beliefs and values. However, a museum exhibit that explains the methods of science more generally may have an impact, if smaller and less direct, since the nature of the topic is less emotionally charged. If the museum-goer walks away with a better understanding of the methods of science, this could contribute to a more open perspective toward climate change research in the future. Other ways to meet participants where they are could involve helping them realize the impact their values have on their beliefs or helping them to learn how to find accurate data on scientific topics. These are examples of incremental steps that may contribute to real impact. Identifying a range of potential incremental goals can help develop engagement activities that are adaptable to participants with different abilities, beliefs, and values.

The fifth strategy we suggest for public-centered engagement involves incorporation of metacognition. Metacognition is the ability to think about thinking, to be consciously aware of oneself as a problem solver, and to monitor and control one's mental processing (Bruer, 1994, p.67). Promoting metacognitive awareness and leveraging participants' motivations enables them to become active participants in the engagement experience. Incorporating awareness of metacognition into one's public engagement practices may enable participants to engage in cognitive acts of meaning-making from experiences and information salient to them. Meaning-making, in this context, is the process whereby participants renovate their existing belief structures toward a coherent worldview given new information. This strategy in the public-centered model of public engagement with science leverages the research behind one of McCombs and Whisler's (1997) student-centered principles, that learning is a constructive process that occurs best when learners can connect new information to existing knowledge.

The sixth strategy we suggest for public-centered engagement is to utilize participant connections. Encourage participants to see one another and themselves as resources and supports for the process in which they are engaging. This strategy reflects the factors McCombs and Whisler (1997) classify as "personal and social." Such factors reflect ways in which others impact the learning process, as learning is not done in isolation. Sharing experiences and building caring and respectful relationships support effective engagement. This includes among public participants, as well as with facilitators of the engagement initiative. As we saw in strategies 1 and 2, the implicit power structures in the traditional deficit model are insufficient for effective belief-value renovation. In the public-centered model, it is critical that participants are seen as individuals with value and potential.

Together, these strategies for public-centered engagement encourage addressing the individual people participating in the engagement activity, including their own relationships to and personal narratives about science. The six strategies are summarized in Table 3. An approach based on these strategies clarifies how a wide range of skills and expertise are relevant to public engagement with science, rather than simply the expertise of scientists who possess the scientific facts. Consider a public engagement initiative focused on the topic of climate change and adaptation. A public audience consisting of well-educated, politically liberal people residing in an urban setting are likely to bring vastly different backgrounds and expectations into engagement on this topic than, say, those who reside in rural settings, are politically conservative, and whose profession, like coal mining, may be in tension with climate adaptation options like renewable energy. Engaging with either group requires attention to interpersonal aspects, perhaps political polarization, identities and worldviews, and personal values and needs tied up in such a topic.

4.2 Integrated Course Design and Goal-Directed Design of Public Engagement

One of the most substantial implications of shifting toward a public-centered conception of public engagement with science is a reassessment of the goals of engagement. The goals of public-centered engagement ought to be heavily influenced by situational factors relating to the participants' beliefs, values, priorities, and connections. This in turn requires a goal-oriented approach to public engagement initiative design. The scholarship of teaching and learning literature has resources to offer for this as well, namely, integrated course design.[10]

Intergraded course design offers a student-centered approach to designing significant learning experiences in educational curriculum contexts. Fink's (2013, p.70) approach to integrated course design poses a series of key questions instructors should answer in order to guide their course development:

1. What are the important *situational factors* in a particular setting and learning situation?
2. What should our *learning goals* be?
3. What kinds *of feedback and assessment* will help us determine that the learning goals are achieved?
4. What kinds of *teaching and learning activities* will support achieving the learning goals?
5. Are all the components *connected and integrated*, that is, are they consistent with and supportive of each other?

We think this sequenced approach of integrated course design also can be productively adopted for developing public engagement with science initiatives. There are three especially important aspects of this approach for a public-centered approach to public engagement with science: the first is related to situational factors, while the second and third relate to learning goals.

First, attending to situational factors effectively is encouraged as a first step in integrated course design (see question 1 above). This first step is crucial for

---

[10] Colloquially, integrated course design and backward course design have become synonymous, with the primary difference of whether the emphasis is placed on sequencing versus integration of addressing the five questions we introduce below. This specific sequencing has been labeled by Wiggins and McTighe (2005) as backward design because step 3 focuses on conceptualizing the conclusion of the learning experience and trying to determine what the learner will have walked away with (which determines the learning goals) and how one might be able to assess whether the learning goals have been achieved. We will simply refer to this as integrated course design. Note, however, that there are distinct literatures on integrated and backward course design. Additionally, note that integrated and backward course design can be applied at multiple scales, from designing courses in their entirety to individual class lesson plans.

public engagement initiatives to achieve their goals. Situational factors are central to strategies 3 and 4 of the public-centered model for public-centered engagement we suggested in the previous section: engaging with participants' belief-value systems and recognizing stages of renovation in learning. Every public engagement encounter will be different, with different relevant situational factors. These situational factors are important to identify and attend to for effective engagement at the front end, with goals and engagement activities selected and developed in response to the situational factors.

To facilitate thinking through relevant situational factors that might impact public engagement goals and activities, it's worth considering the focal questions Fink (2013, pp.76–77) provides for teachers to identify situational factors. These are also applicable for guiding public engagement initiative design. Here is a list of questions to help guide consideration of situational factors; we've modified the questions to apply to public engagement:

- **Specifics about the context in which the engagement will occur:** How big is the group you will interact with? Of what ages and backgrounds? How long and how frequently will you be interacting with them? What constraints are there for the engagement?
- **External expectations:** How could your engagement with this group impact how a broader segment of the public relates to the topic? Why are these public participants interacting with you? Is the interaction intrinsically or instrumentally motivated?
- **The subject you are conducting public engagement about:** Is it convergent, where scientific research provides a correct or best answer, divergent, where the subject enables multiple answers or perspectives, and/or controversial? How can your framing affect whether it's convergent, divergent, or controversial and participants' relationship to the subject?
- **The specific characteristics of the participants:** Different segments of the public are interested in and motivated by different things. Why are the participants there? What do they value? What do they already know or bring with them to the interaction?
- **The characteristics of the person(s) conducting the engagement:** Have they worked with this segment of the public before? What attitudes or preconceptions do they bring about the subject and about the public they are interacting with?
- **The pedagogical challenges:** What makes this specific public engagement encounter unique or challenging?

These questions can help those planning public engagement initiatives reflect in a more robust way on relevant situational factors. This enables their approach to public engagement initiatives to start from consideration of situational factors.

A second aspect of integrated course design that is helpful for developing an effective approach to public engagement is the call for goals to be explicitly articulated, often prior to decisions regarding what activities will be conducted. Question 2 of Fink's approach to integrated course design encourages the consideration of goals immediately after identifying situational factors. Public engagement with science initiatives should start with an explicit articulation of the aims and goals of the initiatives because those aims and goals ought to dictate the features those initiatives should have. Too often, outreach activities of academic researchers are conducted without genuine reflection on and clear articulation of the goals. For public engagement activities, just as for classroom instruction, requiring explicit articulation of aims and goals is a way to keep the "why" front and center in activity design. And then, the remaining questions of Fink's approach indicate how the identified goals drive all other features of the activity design, including assessment as well as the activities themselves.

A third central element of Fink's framework can also be productively applied to public engagement contexts. Recall, in Section 1, we introduced a distinction between aims and goals. We use "aims" to refer to a broad type of targeted outcome of an engagement activity. General aims for public engagement with science we identified include (at least) increased understanding of science, shifted sense of identity, increased trust in science, increased access to participation in science, application of scientific knowledge, and fostering interest in science. These different broad aims in turn lead to initiatives with different specific goals. We urge consideration of broad aims as well as specific goals. Engagement should be directed at broad aims, but accomplishing broad aims requires specifying particular goals. An initiative can't simply aim to shift self-identity, for example. It must also be specified whether the specific goal is to increase recognition of scientists that share participants' backgrounds, to inspire a sense of connection and belonging through the engagement, or something else. Each of these goals may support the aim of shifting self-identity, but they are accomplished in different ways.

Fink identifies six categories of learning goals that, in his view, together comprise significant learning experiences; see Figure 2 (2013, pp.34–28; 83). The categories are (1) foundational knowledge, understanding or remembering specific information or ideas; (2) application, applying facts and ideas to novel scenarios; (3) integration, recognizing connections between different ideas, learning experiences, or even realms of life (such as academic and personal life); (4) human dimension, discovering how to interact more effectively with oneself and

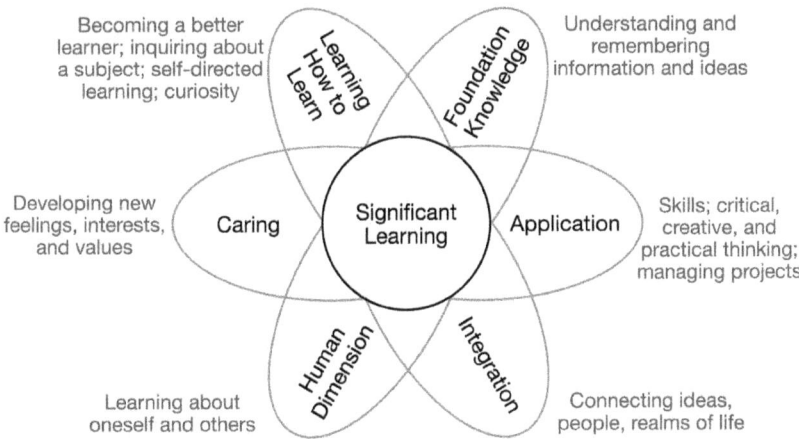

Figure 2 Fink's six categories of significant learning experiences, redrawn from Fink (2013). Reprinted by permission of Informa UK Limited, trading as Taylor & Francis Group, www.tandfonline.com.

others, as when one recognizes societal implications of the ideas; (5) caring, the development of new interests, feelings, or values; and (6) learning how to learn, developing knowledge, skills, or strategies for ongoing learning. Fink notes that a learning experience can have one of these aspects, several aspects, or all six. While having a learning experience focused on one aspect is not problematic, when all six are present and working together, it achieves more significant learning. The six aspects are not considered to be hierarchical, where each must be achieved before the next, but rather relational and interactive.

Fink's six aspects to significant learning experiences to some extent parallel the broad aims for public engagement with science we identified in Section 1; see Table 4. Some engagement efforts might focus on cultivating foundational knowledge. Other efforts might focus the public participants on developing an understanding of how scientific concepts are at play in their own life, paralleling Fink's application and integration. Another aim identified focuses on identity: cultivating a STEM identity, such as seeing STEM as a vocation or career identity, or even seeing science as related to their everyday life. Other aims are to promote having fun related to science and to increase trust in science, perhaps by focusing on relationships, transparency, or justice. These last three types of aims are somewhat aligned with Fink's fourth (human dimension, or interaction), fifth (caring, or developing new feelings, interests, or values), and sixth (learning how to learn) categories of learning.

As Fink emphasizes the value of learning experiences that feature several of the categories he identifies, a successful public engagement initiative may be

Table 4 Parallels between Fink's (2013) categories of significant learning experiences and the aims of public engagement with science we identified in Section 1

Aims of Public Engagement with Science	Fink's Categories of Learning Experiences
Understanding	Foundational knowledge (Understanding and remembering information and ideas)
Interest: Instrumental	Application (skills, critical, creative, practical thinking, managing projects)
Interest: Instrumental; Access; Identity	Integration (Connecting ideas, people, realms of life)
Access; Identity, Trust	Human dimension (Learning about oneself and others)
Identity; Trust; Interest: intrinsic	Caring (developing new feelings, interests, ideas)
Interest: intrinsic; Identity	Learning how to learn (Becoming a better student, inquiring about a subject, self-directed learning)

enriched by attending to how it can address multiple broad aims. An initiative focused on increasing understanding, for instance, may still benefit from addressing aspects of identity or productive use of the knowledge. Depending on the mode of engagement, it's possible to address multiple aims that support one another. For example, consider a public engagement initiative focused on climate change. The initiative could aim to teach about the science of climate change (foundational knowledge) and its local impact in the city (application). However, an additional activity component could allow participants to discuss with each other how they might locally adapt (integration, human dimension) and challenges and questions they have about enacting that change (caring, learning how to learn), which could lead to more significant engagement and enable multiple aims of engagement – understanding, application, and identity – to be addressed.

In this section, we examined three components of intergraded course design that support public-centered public engagement with science: identifying relevant situational factors, establishing learning goals that are informed by those situational factors, and considering how attending to multiple aims may enrich the experience. We discussed how various learning goals may work together to achieve significant learning experiences, and how this parallels the broad aims of public engagement with science efforts. The next section turns to the remaining three components of intergraded course design.

4.3 Integrative Design: Goals, Activities, and Participants

Section 4.2 suggested goal-directed design of public engagement with science initiatives, drawing resources from integrated course design's goal-oriented sequencing. We then addressed how the situational factors and learning goals aspects of integrated course design apply to a public-centered model of public engagement with science. In this final section, we discuss the remaining three aspects of integrated course design. These are captured in Fink's (2013) last three questions:

- What kinds *of feedback and assessment* will help us determine that the learning goals are achieved?
- What kinds of *teaching and learning activities* will support achieving the learning goals?
- Are all the components *connected and integrated*, that is, are they consistent with and supportive of each other?

In integrated course design, only after situational factors and learning goals are determined does one begin to consider what kind of assessment would demonstrate that the students have achieved their learning goals, and what class activities would best support their success with those goals. How do these remaining three questions apply to a public-centered model of public engagement with science?

Fink's fifth question guiding integrated course design stresses the connections among situational factors, learning goals, assessment, and activities. Each of these components is supposed to support the others. Consistent with this integrated approach, we think there are three possible entry points for the decision-making process about how to develop public engagement activities. In brief, it could be the case that one starts with specific goals they wish to achieve by conducting some kind of outreach, with a specific mode of engagement or activity in mind, or by targeting a specific segment of the public to reach as participants. Each of these three starting points of goal, mode of engagement, and participants provides an anchor point that, as we will discuss, in turn has implications for the other two elements. See Figure 3 for a visual representation of these entry points and the ensuing decision-making process.

So far, we have emphasized the advantages of starting with goals first (after considering situational factors). Goal-directed design enables the selection of a mode of engagement and intended participants that are suitable to further one's public cngagement goals. But, in some circumstances, mode of engagement or intended audience is instead a more natural starting point of initiative design. Let's consider each of these in turn.

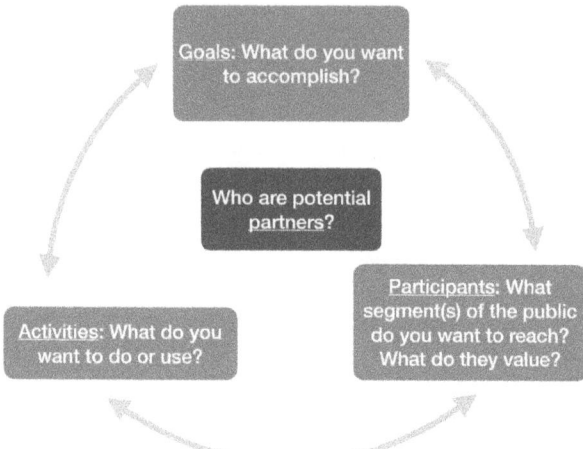

Figure 3 Visual representation of goal-directed design of public engagement with science, integrating consideration of goals, activities, and participants

The modes of engagement or activities in public engagement with science are similar to teaching and learning activities insofar as they are the things participants do or engage in in order to support achieving the established goal(s). Public engagement initiatives can involve a wide variety of different modes of engagement, and these different modes will be better suited to different goals. Modes of engagement can include, for instance, (1) traditional forms of science communication and journalism, like op-eds, public talks, news interviews, websites, and social media; (2) formal science education outreach to K-12 classes or teachers; (3) informal science education, such as activities at museums, zoos, libraries, and parks; (4) scientific research conducted in collaboration with members of the public, such as people volunteering to collect data about the birds in their backyards; and (5) outreach about science policy or to influence public policies. (This delineation of types of public engagement with science initiatives is developed in greater depth in Section 5.)

In some cases, mode of engagement is determined prior to goals or target participants. Sometimes mode of engagement is determined by situational factors. For example, an academic researcher may be invited into a classroom or have an opportunity to write an op-ed for a specific newspaper. Other times, researchers simply have a clear sense of what mode of engagement they prefer. In any case, when mode of engagement is determined first, this constrains what goals are achievable or appropriate. Informal science education, for instance, typically only offers public participants brief encounters with science, but in contexts where they are primed for educational experiences. Many informal settings also attract participants of different ages, from children to adults, each of whom has different backgrounds and interests. In contrast, scientific research conducted in collaboration with public participants may focus on helping to develop greater interest in or understanding of the research topic or of science in general. This setting for public engagement with science provides an opportunity for sustained interactions of researchers and members of the public in a project of shared interest. Different modes of engagement may also bring with them public participants with different features. For example, a classroom invitation determines what age student one will engage with. What we want to stress is that, when the mode of engagement is determined first, goals must be selected in a way that is responsive to that consideration. But by prioritizing connection and integration one can maintain a goal-directed design even in these cases.

The third possible entry point to designing public engagement with science initiatives is selecting a specific segment of the public with which one intends to engage. For example, a researcher might know they would like to do something local in their neighborhood community. This will govern some aspects of the intended audience and will provide the researcher with a way to learn about those audiences. Beginning one's planning with establishing the target participants in turn constrains what modes of engagement and goals are feasible. From what they know about the neighborhood and its existing activities, the researcher can ask who might participate, for what reasons, what they may value, and what situational factors will need to be considered. These considerations should guide what goals are feasible and what modes of engagement may be successful. Starting with a consideration of what segment of the public you want to reach also leads to consideration of whether existing avenues reach this targeted group. In other words, will the intended audience need to be recruited, or is there an existing channel through which they can be reached? Reflection on the values and needs of the targeted segment of the public is critical for determining proper goals and mode of engagement, as values of the public participants may not align with those of the person conducting the public engagement initiative. (See Dunlap et al., 2021 for discussion of the alignment of values and goals in the context of participatory research.)

Regardless of whether the entry point in initiative design is goals, mode of engagement, or intended participants, all three of these features of the project must be intentional, and they must be consistent with and supportive of each other, as called for in Fink's fifth question of integrative design. For public engagement initiatives, another important early question that bears on all other features of the initiative regards community partners. We emphasized the value of partnership with other individuals and organizations in Section 3. It can be extremely beneficial for a public engagement initiative to seek out potential community partners appropriate for the initiative's intended goals, mode of engagement, and desired participants.

Community partners are, in some ways, simply another situational factor: something the designer should take into consideration, as well as a factor that could constrain the goals, mode of engagement, or segment of public one might reach. But community partnerships also provide richer and more meaningful opportunities for engagement through expertise, infrastructure, and access. As we stressed in Section 3, it is important to incorporate input of all partners before finalizing plans for goals, mode, and audiences. Indeed, it is best to include partners at early stages of planning and not simply add their perspectives after plans are nearly finalized. Community partners can help drive, inform, and collaborate on the planned initiative. Placing partnerships at the center of initiative design can thus support all aspects of planning: helping to inform appropriate goals and modes of engagement and to develop a deeper understanding of the targeted segment of the public.

4.4 Engaging Diverse Publics

As we've noted, participants in public engagement activities are not generic "members of the public," but rather individuals with specific social identities, participating in specific communities. Different public engagement with science initiatives will reach different segments of the public. Given some communities' historic exclusion from and even mistreatment by science and medicine, aims of access, identity, and trust will in many cases best be supported by targeting one or more of these communities. More broadly, it is often important to explore more fully which segment(s) of the public is targeted with attention to equity and inclusion, whether the targeted public is an initial choice structuring the engagement or follows from the aims or mode of engagement.

When engaging with the public, we might conceptualize the targeted group or segments of the public in multiple ways. Groups might be targeted by their associations, that is, through formally organized institutions, like clubs, corporations, or political parties. We might also target individuals based on particular attributes, such as gender or age. Or, we might target groups based on a shared sense of identity, such as shared culture, practices, or ways of life. In the context of public outreach and engagement, common types of groupings to target are age (kids, teens, adults), race and ethnicity, gender, cultural community, socioeconomic status or educational attainment (low income, first-generation college students, college graduates, etc.), and identities historically underrepresented in

STEM fields. It's also common to consider freedom in engagement (voluntary, semi-voluntary, required participation).

When the targeted groups include vulnerable social identities – members of underserved communities, people with identities underrepresented in STEM, etc. – these identities must be taken into account for modes of engagement to be effective. For this, culturally relevant pedagogy (CRP), also referred to as culturally sustaining pedagogy or culturally responsive teaching, is another domain in the scholarship of teaching and learning that can be usefully applied to public engagement efforts. Culturally relevant pedagogies, such as those advocated for by Banks (1993), Ladson-Billings (1995, 2023), or Gay (2000, 2018), focus on welcoming and incorporating students' lived experiences, customs, and perspectives in order to collaboratively, in partnership, build educational experiences for increased student engagement and ownership. As Gay (2000) puts it, "when academic knowledge and skills are situated within the lived experiences and frames of reference for students, they are more personally meaningful, have higher interest appeal, and are learned more easily and thoroughly."

Ladson-Billings (1995) identifies three core components of culturally relevant pedagogy. The first is to ensure focus on academic achievement. A teacher's fundamental role is student learning, and so focus should stay on prioritizing the students' intellectual growth and ability to problem-solve. The second is cultivating cultural competencies. Here the idea is that the instructor should acknowledge that culture can impact learning, and so there should be a focus on creating an environment where students affirm and appreciate their culture of origin in learning, while also developing opportunities to learn about other cultures. Finally, CRP focuses on developing critical consciousness. Critical consciousness focuses on teaching students how to identify, analyze, and solve real-world problems, as well as how to identify when those real-world problems are a result of societal inequities for marginalized groups.

Gay (2002) offers guidelines for how to teach in a way aligned with this orientation of CRP. The first is developing one's own cultural diversity knowledge base. It is critical to understand and have knowledge of different cultures, values, and traditions, most critically of groups one teaches or works with. Second is designing culturally relevant curricula, which can include formal lesson plans, symbolic curriculum (such as symbols, icons, examples and imagery), and societal curriculum. Third is demonstrating cultural caring and building a learning community that supports high achievement and enables success for all by providing educational scaffolding for learning about different cultures. Fourth is an appreciation for and literacy in different communication styles (for example, what might be taken as a rude or dismissive way to engage in conversation in one culture might be standard within another). Finally, cultural congruity in classroom instruction connects students' prior knowledge and cultural experiences with the new knowledge they are learning.

In considering how CRP applies in the context of public engagement with science, it is worth highlighting a few points. First, a focus on CRP does not involve assimilating one culture into the norms and standards of the other. Rather, the focus is on making space for and connections between groups that may have different cultures. This involves not only learning more about the public you wish to engage with but also reflecting on one's own identity in relation to that public. Second, just as culture impacts learning (Hammond, 2014), we should reflect on how the cultures of our targeted participants may impact our modes of achieving our public engagement goals. Different techniques will be more effective when targeting different communities. One ought to consider also how targeting particular groups may influence other features of the engagement. Practices of inclusive pedagogy are especially relevant (Jacquart et al., 2019), as is work on intercultural teaching competence (Dimitrov and Haque, 2016).

The application of culturally relevant pedagogy in STEM education contexts is an excellent space to look to for resources that may be applicable to public engagement with science efforts. For example, Kayumova (2022), McKinley and Gan (2014), Smith et al. (2022), and Thevenot (2022) offer conceptual frameworks and advice for implementing culturally responsive and sustaining STEM curriculums. For those looking for example teaching tools specifically, https://stemteachingtools.org has a number of briefings on the topic (see especially brief 31, 53, and 58). Also, https://cadrek12.org offers videos and resources, including, for instance, videos on culturally responsive science education as well as rural partnerships.

4.5 Implementing Integrated, Goal-Directed Design

In this section, we have suggested resources from the scholarship on teaching and learning that may be useful for planning public engagement with science initiatives. To start, insights from student-centered learning can be reapplied to engaging with public participants, influencing the goals of that engagement by centering participant needs and interests and engaging with them as unique individuals. And then, integrated course design can be used to inspire a goal-directed approach to public engagement with science initiatives. Initiative design should start from consideration of goals and situational factors, and then approach decisions about activities and participants with that perspective in mind. For public engagement, a consideration of community partners is also integral to establishing a cohesive plan of mutually supportive goals, participants, and activities. Public engagement with science initiatives, like curriculum design, benefit from intentional, goal-directed design.

One final application of integrated course design is to evaluation or assessment (following Fink's fourth question, as listed above).[11] It's important to consider, beginning at an early stage of planning, how one might evaluate if an initiative's goals have been achieved, and how evaluation needs should influence initiative design. Evaluation of public engagement with science initiatives may be more challenging than assessment in formal education, as there may not be a clear opportunity for evaluation akin to graded assignments. Consider, for example, producing an op-ed piece advocating for a certain lifestyle change in response to climate change. The author may have written the piece with the concrete goal of convincing people to make that lifestyle change, but it will be hard to measure the impact of this op-ed piece on achieving this goal. For some initiatives, measures of success may be limited to tracking how many people have engaged, or whether they report enjoying their experience.

Nonetheless, planning and executing evaluation of an initiative is essential for establishing if the initiative's goal has been achieved. Further, planning evaluation is an important opportunity to reflect on the alignment of goals, mode of engagement, and intended participants. If a public engagement with science initiative seeks to change participants' perspectives or values, for example, strategic thinking is required to consider how to evaluate changed perspectives or values. As with integrated course design, careful consideration of all aspects of public engagement initiatives together – goals, activities, participants, partners, and evaluation – can strengthen and increase the meaningfulness of the engagement. To support effective evaluation, consider partnering with academics or professionals with expertise in educational evaluation or educational research. Friedman (2008), Frechtling (2010), and CAISE (2011) provide introductory guides to evaluation in informal education.

An appendix to this Element provides a series of questions to guide someone through this goal-oriented approach to designing public engagement with science initiatives. The main ideas from this section to consider employing are, first, to design initiatives that empower, respect, and engage with participants – participant-centered design – and, second, to engage in integrative planning. This means taking

---

[11] In this context, the terms "evaluation" and "assessment" are sometimes used interchangeably but also can have specific, different meanings. "Assessment" is most often used to refer to assessment of individuals' educational outcomes, as with exams, while "evaluation" is most often used to refer to evaluating the success of an intervention or program (in general, not linked to individual student outcomes). While assessments are focal in the pedagogical literatures we're drawing from in this section, program evaluation is most applicable to public engagement with science initiatives. Note that sometimes participant assessments can play a role in initiative evaluation, but they may not.

a goal-directed approach, while considering constraints of the mode of engagement, intended participants, and partners. Starting from a consideration of goals and situational factors and only then beginning to consider what you will *do* for engagement leads to more impactful initiatives. And considering potential approaches to evaluation as you design will enable you to demonstrate that impact.

5 Conducting, Teaching, and Researching Public Engagement with Science

So far, we have identified what we mean by public engagement with science (Section 1), described the disciplines that have expertise to offer public engagement with science (Section 2), discussed the institutional structures and collaborations that can support public engagement with science (Section 3), and described resources from the scholarship of teaching and learning that can support public-centered and goal-directed public engagement with science (Section 4).

In this final section, we describe a range of outreach activities comprising public engagement with science, providing a taxonomy of types based on their format and context. The aim of doing so is to illustrate the wide variety of formats of public engagement with science and provide fodder for readers interested to newly develop or differently situate their engagement activities. Then, we conclude this Element by discussing the need for formal instruction and interdisciplinary research targeting public engagement with science. Together, these topics can be summarized as an overview of conducting, teaching, and researching public engagement with science.

5.1 Public Engagement with Science Activities

In this section, we develop a loose taxonomy of types of public engagement with science activities based on their format and context. These types of activities are what we referred to in Section 4 as modes of engagement. It's beyond the scope of this Element to provide guidance on how to conduct activities of these kinds; that is the focus of another forthcoming Element in this series, *A Guide for Academic Researchers Conducting Public Engagement with Science*. The present focus is simply cataloging types of public engagement and how they vary from one another.

Science Communication. When university-based academics are motivated to engage with the public, oftentimes the first activities that occur to them relate to public talks and writing. This is natural. For one thing, academics are trained in writing and public speaking and are well versed in writing and speaking about their research. Speaking and writing for public audiences requires different content and strategies from academic communication, but these are a natural expansion of familiar activities. A common name for these activities is *science communication*. As we noted in Section 2, science communication activities are often carried out without attention to the fields of journalism or science communication that we surveyed in that section. There is an opportunity to enrich such approaches by attending to relevant disciplinary research.

Science communication activities include giving talks for the public, writing op-eds for newspapers with local or national audiences, longer-form public writing including trade books, media interviews, and even social media activity. Public audiences have different backgrounds, knowledge, and interests than a typical academic audience, and different segments of the public differ in these respects from one another. Effectively engaging with these audiences requires sensitivity to these differences. Each format of science communication activities also comes with its own localized norms and expectations.

Formal Education. For many people, much of their experience engaging with scientific knowledge occurs as part of their formal education – K-12 and, for many, also in collegiate education. Activities in collegiate education settings may not seem like public engagement, as college instruction is part of many academics' job descriptions. Nonetheless, collegiate audiences are easy to access and an important opportunity to influence students' relationship to science in ways that may last long into their lives after college. As Editor-in-Chief of the journal *Science*, H. Holden Thorp (2024) has touted the importance of this variety of public engagement. General education college classes offer a key opportunity to further many of the aims of public engagement with science, including especially understanding, identity, and trust. Further, college classroom engagement benefits from some of the same theoretical and practical resources as other forms of public engagement with science.

Outreach in K-12 classroom settings, and even preschool, also can be opportunities to influence students' understanding of science and trust and identity as well. These settings are in some regards similar to collegiate instruction, which academic researchers tend to be familiar with, though it should be stressed that many features of K-12 teaching are different from collegiate teaching. Public engagement with science activities in a formal education context may be brief, as with classroom visits and facilitated activities like hosting school fieldtrips, or they might be extended, such as extended engagement with one class or the development of new curricula. An important opportunity for collaborative, interdisciplinary public engagement with science is also created in teacher enrichment and continuing education trainings.

Informal Education. Learning about science also occurs beyond the traditional classroom. Informal and non-formal science education, such as in museums, zoos, libraries, and parks, offers members of the public relatively brief encounters with science in contexts where they are primed for educational experiences. Many informal education settings also attract an audience of different ages, from children to adults, with a broad variety of backgrounds and interests. Many informal education organizations and venues regularly seek programming, which is a key opportunity for one-off or sustained initiatives. Science-focused organizations like zoos and museums are an obvious opportunity, but other informal education settings, like libraries, youth centers, and parks are often also interested in science programming.

Public engagement with science initiatives in informal science education settings may involve contributions to exhibitions, such as contributing to textual resources accompanying physical artifacts, or in live interactions with visitors, such as serving as a practicing scientist in an open lab in a science museum or guiding an interactive activity. Some opportunities in these spaces look more like science communication, such as public talks and panel discussions.

Public Participation in Research. The types of public engagement with science cataloged so far focus on educational aims, promoting understanding, learning, and interest, and perhaps also cultivating science-positive identities and trust in science. A different kind of opportunity for public engagement with science presents itself with the inclusion of public participants in scientific research, such as people volunteering to collect data about the birds in their backyard or a high-school class providing local ecological data. A related form of engagement is working to cultivate support for, for example, medical research and underrepresented communities' participation as research subjects.

Public participation in scientific research is an opportunity to further aims of understanding the research and the process of conducting scientific research, to cultivate interest in scientific research and identities with positive relationships to STEM, as well as increased trust and, perhaps especially for health research and local environmental research, individual and community access to the insights that scientific inquiry can provide. In some cases, this form of public engagement with science provides an opportunity for sustained interactions of researchers and public participants in a project of shared interest. Public participation in research ranges from public involvement in data collection, to the inclusion of members of the public as co-researchers who influence all aspects of research design and data collection and analysis, to community leaders initiating their own scientific research and then soliciting the involvement of professional scientists (Shirk et al., 2012).

Science Policy. Yet another variety of public engagement with science targets policymakers or public understanding of policy. Scientific research in a wide range of fields has potential implications for public policy. An important variety of public engagement with science targets the specific segment of the public consisting of policymakers – local, state, or national – in order to inform them about relevant research in an attempt to influence their perspectives on policy. For example, a college class focused on local climate change impacts may present their findings to the local city council, attempting to influence local policy or the priority councilmembers place on climate mitigation and adaptation. Science policy outreach may also occur in collaboration with relevant nonprofit organizations, such as sustainability- or health-care-focused groups. Further, some science policy efforts do not target policymakers but the broader public, with the goal of improving public understanding of some policy implication, science-based public advocacy about policy decisions, or gathering public input in the policymaking process.

As this discussion has suggested, the categories we have introduced here are not entirely distinct types of public engagement with science but partially overlapping. What distinguishes the categories from one another are differences in typical modes of engagement, to some extent differences in the typical segments of the public reached, both of which (as we have seen in Section 4) may influence the goals of engagement. See Table 5 for an overview of the differences.

It's worth considering how this list of types of public engagement with science initiatives relates to other taxonomies. AAAS (2016) provides a literature analysis to yield a typology of five types of public engagement with science, with variations within each:

1. Deliberative – usually tied to policy and directly addressing issues at the intersection of science and society; outcomes directly tied to policy action are most common;
2. Dialogue – somewhat more process-based, with the act of interaction driving its definition; outcomes tend toward more personal-level changes in interest, affect, or knowledge;
3. Knowledge Co-Production – emphasis on the process of science; outcomes relate to building scientific skills in publics and bringing nonexpert perspectives to research;
4. University-Led Cooperative – focuses on professional communities and how university researchers can provide expert consultation and collaboration to support their efforts;
5. Informal – informal one-on-one interactions in daily life between scientists and publics; primarily neglected in the literature, this category represents (likely) the most frequently experienced and least studied type of engagement.

Table 5 Five types of public engagement with science initiatives

Engagement Type	Key Features	Sample Activities
Science Communication	Written or oral communication about scientific topics intended for public audiences	Op-eds and essays Public talks and panels Trade books Media requests and interviews Social media activity
Formal Education	Engagement targeting K-12 or collegiate classes or teachers	Classroom visits and fieldtrips Extended classroom projects Curricula or teacher resources
Informal Education	Engagement targeting informal education spaces like museums, zoos, libraries, and parks	Exhibition contributions Scientific research in open lab Hands-on activities Panels and talks
Public Participation in Research	Inclusion of public in research activities or advocacy of research involvement	Public participation in data collection Participatory research influenced by community concerns Outreach about research involvement
Science policy	Engagement targeting policy outcomes or use of scientific research findings in policymaking	Meetings with policymakers (local, state, or national) Collaboration with stakeholders on reports for policymakers Public outreach about policy

A full analysis of this taxonomy is beyond the scope of this Element, but a few comments are worth making. These five types are primarily defined by different goals, respectively: scientific influence on public policy and norms (deliberative); scientific influence on public interest, affect, knowledge (dialogue); public influence on scientific research (knowledge co-production), scientific support for public goals (university-led cooperative), and casual personal interactions that are not goal driven (what the AAAS typology calls "informal"; note that this is different than what we've referred to as informal science education). Our list of public engagement types is not linked to goals in this straightforward way. We see the primary delineators as the mode of engagement and typical audience(s) reached through that format. The general aims and specific goals may vary and there may be multiple goals for any one initiative. Further, we believe the goals of public engagement with science initiatives should usually be more bidirectional than this AAAS typology suggests. That said, this taxonomy does capture some important differences in goals and processes of public engagement initiatives. It is probably useful to consider multiple characterizations of public engagement with science types as one considers how to develop such initiatives.

AAAS (2016) also notes that any of these forms of engagement can occur in person or virtually, with the latter increasingly common for public engagement. It is certainly true that, as virtual communication becomes ever-more prevalent, virtual public engagement becomes more common. Virtual engagement offers some new opportunities: to reach larger audiences, unconstrained by geographic location; to host resources that are available on demand; and to innovate with creative new approaches to engagement. It's also worth noting, though, that for many goals, localized, in-person engagement offers advantages in both partnership formation and relationship development over virtual public engagement. In many cases, it's also easier to engage in bidirectional or multidirectional influence – with outreach goals of not simply reaching the public participants but of improving one's own understanding or connection in the process – in live, in-person encounters rather than in creating content for virtual consumption.

5.2 Teaching Public Engagement with Science

Training in public engagement with science has a real potential to improve graduate education in the sciences and allied fields – and perhaps undergraduate collegiate education as well. Academic scientists face mounting pressure to carry out research with meaningful broader impacts and to engage with the public about their research. Moreover, as the availability of traditional academic science jobs decreases, graduate students in the sciences need to be trained in a way that more effectively prepares them for a variety of careers related to science, including but not limited to industry, technology, and nonprofit settings. Yet many graduate students emerging from traditional STEM programs need supplementary preparation to fully capitalize on such opportunities. Skills in public engagement with science thus should be more meaningfully integrated into STEM graduate education. The pedagogical advantages of sustained, strategic instruction are clearly established (e.g. Brown, 2014). And, as we have seen above, public engagement with science instruction must address complex issues like trust in science, political polarization, differences in identities and worldviews, and understanding scientific methods and social structure.

Research shows that today's graduate students have a strong and growing interest in public engagement with science (Eatman, 2012; Jaeger et al., 2014; Clarkson et al., 2018). Systematic instruction in public engagement with science can enable graduate students to develop better research, teaching, and communication skills; to connect to public audiences and organizations in ways that enrich their education; and to acquire knowledge about their own disciplines in ways that deepens understanding. This can set students up for more engaged and rewarding careers in science, and it can also prepare students for a broader range of career opportunities – in scientific roles outside the academy, community nonprofit organizations, policy, and much more. Moreover, by engaging with the public, students may come to view public engagement with science less as a unidirectional process characterized by disseminating research findings and more as a dynamic process of exchange characterized by bidirectional communication and deeper engagement.

Public engagement with science training is also well positioned to support diversity and inclusion in STEM. One of the well-documented barriers to recruitment and retention of underrepresented students in STEM is a lack of a sense of belonging. Recent work indicates that efforts to foster a STEM identity can improve retention and career outcomes, particularly for underrepresented students (Lane, 2017). Moreover, a public engagement with science training program may support graduate students' sense of belonging (Rainey et al., 2018) and the alignment of STEM education with their goals (Diekman et al., 2017), such that they feel a part of a community of public engagement with science scholars whose research can have a societal impact. Further, public engagement with science includes a focus on the social context of science and science's societal impact. Such an emphasis enables students to see how their work can matter to society at large and to particular communities.

In short, public engagement with science training may be a valuable opportunity in collegiate settings, especially – but not only – for graduate students in STEM disciplines. In line with the range of disciplinary resources that can inform public engagement with science efforts, as outlined in Section 2, such instruction is likely to benefit from an interdisciplinary approach. Further, just as public engagement initiatives benefit from community partnership, insight from professionals in this space can be incredibly important for effective training opportunities in public engagement. We hope that this Element – and the interdisciplinary series it initiates – will be useful for such instruction.

Such training opportunities may take the form of new collegiate courses, but there are a variety of other opportunities to provide college students with opportunities for learning about public engagement. Course designations like service learning and applied research can provide opportunities to involve public engagement with science initiatives in existing courses. A course may ask students to work in teams or as a class to conduct community research, to present findings to local policymakers, or to engage with a local museum. A different opportunity to offer training in public engagement with science may be including interested students in your planned initiatives, or later scaling those initiatives to include student participation. This can include paid student worker or internship opportunities if resources are available. Students can also help in establishing relationships with community partner organizations, learning valuable skills and of potential career paths in the process.

5.3 Interdisciplinary Research on Public Engagement with Science

Just as training in public engagement with science is well positioned to enrich collegiate education, especially of graduate students in STEM disciplines, so too is public engagement with science a worthy target for academic research. Of course, as outlined in Section 2, research in a number of existing disciplines bears on public engagement with science, some – like science communication and science education – quite directly. Still, researchers from a variety of academic disciplines conduct public engagement with science of one type or another, often with little awareness of or influence from these disciplinary resources. This circumstance presents an opportunity, first, to better connect researchers across disciplines to disciplinary research bearing on public engagement and, second, to expand interdisciplinary research that can inform public engagement activities.

We hope the series this Element initiates can help accomplish both of those ends. The series, Elements in Public Engagement with Science, aims to be an interdisciplinary exploration of academic research and professional expertise related to interfaces between science and the public. Its aim is to make accessible to a broader audience of academics and public engagement professionals specialized knowledge bearing on public engagement with science, as well as ground-breaking research in areas of public engagement with science. This series anticipates that treating topics like science communication, formal and informal science education, community participation in scientific research, science policy, and other interfaces between science and the public alongside one another in an interdisciplinary forum will advance both theory and practice of public engagement with science.

Beyond Section 2's survey of disciplinary resources bearing on public engagement with science, it will be useful to briefly highlight some of the main cross-disciplinary resources that can support efforts in public engagement. To start, the American Academy for the Advancement of Science (AAAS), which we have referred to periodically through this Element, offers a robust set of guidelines, trainings, and opportunities for public engagement with science; see the AAAS website (https://www.aaas.org/programs/public-engagement) for more information. *Public Understanding of Science* is an interdisciplinary academic journal examining how science relates to the public across different societies. Research and discussion of public engagement with science also sometimes crops up in generalist academic science journals, like *Science, Nature, Proceedings of the National Academy of Sciences*, and *PLOSOne*, among others. The National Informal STEM Education Network, or NISE Network, develops educational materials and professional training in informal science education; many resources are available on the NISE Network website (https://www.nisenet.org). REVISE, Reimagining Equity and Value in Informal STEM Education, hosts resources for research and evaluation on informal science learning: https://informalscience.org/repository/. The Association for Advancing Participatory Sciences offers online resources for including the public in scientific research: https://participatorysciences.org/resources/. Of course, this is far from a comprehensive list of resources, but it provides some starting points for researchers interested to explore the research on public engagement with science, regardless of their disciplinary background.

A concern sometimes raised about cross-disciplinary pursuits is that the pursuits become vague and ill-defined in virtue of lacking a disciplinary home. And, indeed, exactly this concern has been raised about public engagement with science. It has been suggested that "public engagement with science" is a vague buzzword without meaning (Bensaude-Vincent, 2014; Weingart et al., 2021). Focusing their discussion on science communication and science policy literatures, Weingart et al., suggest that both the public that is reached and the nature of the engagement are increasingly vague, including many different public targets and many different forms of engagement. This is consistent with our emphasis that "public engagement with science" is an umbrella term, with different applications. But Weingart and Connoway see that as part of the problem:

> The vagueness amongst science communication scholars and science policymakers regarding the most appropriate formats, features and objectives of public engagement with science is striking. It is apparent in the virtual absence of any clear definition of what "engagement" is supposed to mean. The characterizations as "an umbrella term" and "an overarching term" in both the academic and political rhetoric, amount to an effective surrender to the plethora of meanings, interpretations and activities that are all seeking inclusion in the popular appeal of the buzz (Weingart et al., 2021).

Though a positive proposal is not a focus of their article, the authors do suggest in passing, as an alternative to public engagement with science, "communication and engagement with clearly defined stakeholder groups about specific problems and the pertinent scientific knowledge."

We believe this concern of vagueness and emptiness is worth attending to. There is always some risk of obfuscation and empty rhetoric when developing pursuits that transcend disciplinary boundaries and create large umbrella categories, and attending to this concern can help shed light on why interdisciplinary research (and training) in public engagement with science is important. Sustained research regarding what the category of public engagement with science amounts to, what commonalities exist across these pursuits, theoretical and practical resources for conducting public engagement with science, and empirical research about public engagement's purposes and successes can help clarify and refine public engagement with science as a set of activities and as a target of inquiry. Further, Weingart and collaborators are surely correct that it is crucial to clearly specify the goal of and identify the relevant segment of the public for any given public engagement with science initiative. This has been an emphasis of our Element, especially in Section 4.

It is unquestionable that, as we pointed out at the beginning of this Element, there are many interfaces between science and the public. Scientific institutions and the public need to engage with each other in a variety of ways. What remains an open question – and that warrants additional research in a variety of forms – is the extent to which engaging with those interfaces takes common forms and is benefited from common approaches, and what the benefits are of such engagement. This Element, and the series to follow, aims to contribute to the productive exploration of these and related questions.

Appendix: Guide for Designing a Public Engagement with Science Initiative

Getting Started: Orienting Questions + Identifying Partners

- What are your specific **goals** for the initiative?
  How do your goals relate to the broader aims of understanding, identity, trust, access, instrumental interest, or intrinsic interest? Are the goals achievable for your audience and mode of engagement?
- Who is the intended **public**?
  What do you know about them? What do they need? What do they value? What relevant situational factors will you need to account for? Will you need to recruit the participants? What kinds of participants enable the goals and mode of engagement you have in mind?
- What do you know about your **mode of engagement**?
  What do you want participants to do? How long will the encounter be, and will there be repeat encounters? Can there be audience engagement or only one-way communication? What situational factors are relevant? What mode of engagement is appropriate for your intended participants and goals?
- Who are potential **community partners**?
  What are their priorities and how do they align with yours? What have they already done? What might they know about the participants? What benefits and costs will the initiative have for them?

Implementation

- How do your answers to the questions above shape your **engagement activity**?
  What might be some potential engagement activities? How do these potential activities achieve your goals with the participants you are targeting? What questions do you have that would inform your plan?
- What are your **implementation plans**?
  Plan out all the details: Advertisement and recruitment; registration or sign-in for data/evaluation; materials; game plan; pre-meetings with partners; follow-up and potential for continuity/scaling. What challenges might arise for planning or implementing your initiative?

Evaluation and Follow-up

- How will you know if your goals have been achieved? How will you define and **evaluate success**?
- How will you **follow up** with participants and with partners after implementing the initiative?
- What is the potential for **continuing or scaling** the initiative?

Make It Happen

Consider what you know about goals, public, mode of engagement, potential partners, and potential implementation plans.

- What **questions** do you have about your engagement activity plans?
- How could you pursue getting **answers** to these questions?
- What are **4–7 actionable steps** you need to take to begin the initiative?
- What **timeline and target dates** will you set for yourself?

References

Adams, Melanie A., 2017. Deconstructing systems of bias in the museum field using critical race theory. *Journal of Museum Education*, *42*(3), pp.290–295.

Agate, N., Long, C. P., Russell, B. et al., 2022. *Walking the talk: Toward a values-aligned academy.* The HuMetricsHSS Team. https://doi.org/10.17613/06sf-ad45.

Allum, N., Sturgis, P., Tabourazi, D. and Brunton-Smith, I., 2008. Science knowledge and attitudes across cultures: A meta-analysis. *Public Understanding of Science*, *17*(1), pp.35–54.

Alpert, C. L., 2009. Broadening and deepening the impact: A theoretical framework for partnerships between science museums and STEM research centres. *Social Epistemology*, *23*(3–4), pp.267–281.

Alsan, M. and Wanamaker, M., 2018. Tuskegee and the health of black men. *The Quarterly Journal of Economics*, *133*(1), pp.407–455.

American Association for the Advancement of Science (AAAS). 2016. *Theory of Change for Public Engagement with Science.* AAAS, pp.1–12. www.aaas.org/sites/default/files/content_files/2016-09-15_PES_Theory-of-Change-for-Public-Engagement-with-Science_Final.pdf.

American Physical Society. 2007. APS News. (Volume 16, Number 6). www.aps.org/publications/apsnews/200706/nsf.cfm.

Armstrong, A. K., Krasny, M. E. and Schuldt, J. P. 2018. *Communicating climate change: A guide for educators.* Cornell University Press.

Banks, J. A., 1993. Multicultural education: Historical development, dimensions, and practice. *Review of Research in Education*, *19*, pp.3–49.

Barr, R. B. and Tagg, J., 1995. From teaching to learning – A new paradigm for undergraduate education. *Change: The Magazine of Higher Learning*, *27*(6), pp.12–26.

Basu, S. J. and Barton, A. C., 2010. A researcher-student-teacher model for democratic science pedagogy: Connections to community, shared authority, and critical science agency. *Equity & Excellence in Education*, *43*(1), pp.72–87.

Bayer, R. and Fairchild, A. L., 2004. The genesis of public health ethics. *Bioethics*, *18*(6), pp.473–492.

Becker, K. H. and Park, K., 2011. Integrative approaches among science, technology, engineering, and mathematics (STEM) subjects on students' learning: A meta-analysis. *Journal of STEM Education: Innovations and Research*, *12*(5), pp. 23–37.

Bensaude-Vincent, B. 2014. The politics of buzzwords at the interface of technoscience, market and society: The case of "public engagement in science." *Public Understanding of Science, 23*(3), pp.238–253.

Besley, J. C., Dudo, A. and Storksdieck, M., 2015. Scientists' views about communication training. *Journal of Research in Science Teaching, 52*(2), pp.199–220.

Bornmann, L., 2013. What is societal impact of research and how can it be assessed? A literature survey. *Journal of the American Society for Information Science and Technology, 64*(2), pp.217–233.

Borrego, M. and Newswander, L. K., 2010. Definitions of interdisciplinary research: Toward graduate-level interdisciplinary learning outcomes. *The Review of Higher Education, 34*(1), pp.61–84.

Bozeman, B. and Boardman, C., 2009. Broad impacts and narrow perspectives: Passing the buck on science and social impacts. *Social Epistemology, 23* (3–4), pp.183–198.

Brown, P. C. 2014. *Make it stick*. Harvard University Press.

Bruer, J. T., 1994. *Schools for thought: A science of learning in the classroom*. MIT press.

Burke, A., Okrent, A. and Hale, K., 2022. The State of U.S. Science and Engineering 2022. National Science Board, pp. 1–48. https://ncses.nsf.gov/pubs/nsb20221/.

Burns, T. W., O'Connor, D. J. and Stocklmayer, S. M. 2003. Science communication: A contemporary definition. *Public Understanding of Science, 12*, pp.183–202. https://doi.org/10.1177/09636625030122004.

Campbell, W. E. and Smith, K. A. Eds., 1997. *New paradigms for college teaching*. Interaction Book.

Cat, J., 2023. Otto Neurath, *The Stanford Encyclopedia of Philosophy* (Spring Edition), Edward N. Zalta and Uri Nodelman (Eds.), https://plato.stanford.edu/archives/spr2023/entries/neurath/.

Center for Advancement of Informal Science Education (CAISE). 2011. Principal Investigator's Guide: Managing Evaluation in Informal STEM Education Projects. Washington, DC: cai. http://informalscience.org/evaluation/evaluation-resources/pi-guide.

Chang, H., 2011. How historical experiments can improve scientific knowledge and science education: The cases of boiling water and electrochemistry. *Science & Education, 20*, pp.317–341.

Clarkson, M. D., Houghton, J., Chen, W. and Rohde, J. (2018). Speaking about science: A student-led training program improves graduate students' skills in public communication. *Journal of Science Communication, 17*(2), A05.

de Melo-Martín, I. and Intemann, K., 2018. *The fight against doubt: How to bridge the gap between scientists and the public*. Oxford University Press.

Derrick, E. G., Falk-Krzesinski, H. J., Roberts, M. R. and Olson, S., 2011. Facilitating interdisciplinary research and education: A practical guide. In *report from the "Science on FIRE: Facilitating Interdisciplinary Research and Education" workshop of the American Association for the Advancement of Science*.

Diekman, A. B., Steinberg, M., Brown, E. R., Belanger, A. L. and Clark, E. K., 2017. A goal congruity model of role entry, engagement, and exit: Understanding communal goal processes in STEM gender gaps. *Personality and Social Psychology Review*, *21*(2), pp.142–175.

Dimitrov, N. and Haque, A. (2016). Intercultural teaching competence: A multidisciplinary framework for instructor reflection. *Intercultural Education: Learning at Intercultural Intersections*. *27*(5), pp.437–456. https://doi.org/10.1080/14675986.2016.1240502.

Dimitrov, N. and Haque, A. (2016). Intercultural teaching competence in the disciplines. In Pérez, G. M. G. and Rojas-Primus, C. (Eds.), *Promoting intercultural communication competencies in higher education* (pp. 89–119). IGI Global. https://ir.lib.uwo.ca/ctlpub/16/.

Dunlap, L., Corris, A., Jacquart, M., Biener, Z. and Potochnik, A., 2021. Divergence of values and goals in participatory research. *Studies in History and Philosophy of Science*, *88*, pp.284–291.

Eatman, T. K., 2012. The arc of the academic career bends toward publicly engaged scholarship. In Gilvin, A., Robers, G. M. and Martin, C., (Eds.), *Collaborative futures: Critical reflections on publicly active graduate education*. Syracuse University Press, pp. 25–48.

Falk, J. H. and Dierking, L. D., 2010. The 95 percent solution. *American Scientist*, *98*(6), pp.486–493.

Fealing, K. H., Lane, J. I., Marburgher III, J. H. and Shipp, S. S. Eds., 2011. *The science of science policy: A handbook*. Stanford University Press.

Feinstein, N., 2011. Salvaging science literacy. *Science education*, *95*(1), pp.168–185.

Fink, L. D., 2013. *Creating significant learning experiences: An integrated approach to designing college courses*. John Wiley & Sons.

Fischhoff, B. and Scheufele, D. A., 2013. The science of science communication. *Proceedings of the National Academy of Sciences*, *110*(supplement_3), pp.14031–14032.

Fracchiolla, C., 2023. The power of outreach. *Science (New York, NY)*, *380* (6646), pp.766–766.

Frechtling, J., 2010. *The 2010 user-friendly handbook for project evaluation*. Westat for the National Science Foundation Directorate for Education and Human Resources.

Freire, P., 1970. *Pedagogy of the Oppressed*. Continuum, New York.

Friedman, A. J. Ed., 2008. Framework for Evaluating Impacts of Informal Science Education Projects. Report from a National Science Foundation Workshop. https://informalscience.org/research/framework-evaluating-impacts-informal-science-education-projects/.

Fritzsche, S., Hart-Davidson, W. and Long, C. P., 2022. Charting pathways of intellectual leadership: An initiative for transformative personal and institutional change. *Change: The Magazine of Higher Learning*, *54*(3), pp.19–27.

Frodeman, R. and Holbrook, J. B., 2011. NSF's struggle to articulate relevance. *Science*, *333*(6039), pp.157–158.

Fry, R., Kennedy, B. and Funk, C., 2021. STEM jobs see uneven progress in increasing gender, racial and ethnic diversity. *Pew Research Center*, pp.1–28. www.pewresearch.org/science/wp-content/uploads/sites/16/2021/03/PS_2021.04.01_diversity-in-STEM_REPORT.pdf.

Funk, C., Kennedy, B. and Johnson, C., 2020. Trust in medical scientists has grown in US, but mainly among democrats. *Pew Research Center*, pp.1–43. www.pewresearch.org/science/wp-content/uploads/sites/16/2020/05/PS_2020.05.21_trust-in-scientists_REPORT.pdf.

Garik, P. and Benétreau-Dupin, Y., 2014. Report on a Boston University conference December 7–8, 2012 on how can the history and philosophy of science contribute to contemporary US science teaching? *Science & Education*, *23*, pp.1853–1873.

Garik, P., Garbayo, L., Benétreau-Dupin, Y. et al. 2015. Teaching the conceptual history of physics to physics teachers. *Science & Education*, *24*, pp.387–408.

Gay, G., 2002. Preparing for culturally responsive teaching. *Journal of Teacher Education*, *53*(2), pp.106–116.

Gay, G., 2018. *Culturally responsive teaching: Theory, research, and practice*. Teachers College Press.

Gay, G. and Howard, T. C., 2000. Multicultural teacher education for the 21st century. *The Teacher Educator*, *36*(1), pp.1–16.

Goldberg, M. H. and Gustafson, A., 2023. A framework for understanding the effects of strategic communication campaigns. *International Journal of Strategic Communication*, *17*(1), pp. 1–20.

Goldenberg, M. J., 2021. *Vaccine hesitancy: Public trust, expertise, and the war on science*. University of Pittsburgh Press.

Groffman, P. M., Stylinski, C., Nisbet, M. C. et al., 2010. Restarting the conversation: Challenges at the interface between ecology and society. *Frontiers in Ecology and the Environment*, *8*(6), pp.284–291.

Gunawardena, S., Weber, R. and Agosto, D. E., 2010. Finding that special someone: Interdisciplinary collaboration in an academic context. *Journal of Education for Library and Information Science*, *51*(4), pp.210–221.

Gutstein, E., 2007. "And that's just how it starts": Teaching mathematics and developing student agency. *Teachers College Record*, *109*(2), pp.420–448.

Hammond, Z., 2014. *Culturally responsive teaching and the brain: Promoting authentic engagement and rigor among culturally and linguistically diverse students*. Corwin Press.

Harry, B. and Klingner, J., 2007. Discarding the deficit model. *Educational Leadership*, *64*(5), p. 16.

Hess, D. J., 1997. *Science studies: An advanced introduction*. NYU press.

Hong, H. Y. and Lin-Siegler, X., 2012. How learning about scientists' struggles influences students' interest and learning in physics. *Journal of Educational Psychology*, *104*(2), p.469.

Hooks, b., 1994. *Teaching to transgress*. Routledge.

Hooks, b., 2003. *Teaching community: A pedagogy of hope*. Routledge.

Hubbs, G., O'Rourke, M. and Orzack, S. H. Eds., 2020. *The toolbox dialogue initiative: The power of cross-disciplinary practice*. CRC Press.

Iltis, A. S. and MacKay, D. Eds., 2020. *The oxford handbook of research ethics*. Oxford University Press. https://doi.org/10.1093/oxfordhb/9780190947750.001.0001.

Jacquart, M., Scott, R., Hermberg, K., and Bloch-Schulman, S. (2019). Diversity is not enough: The importance of inclusive pedagogy. *Teaching Philosophy*, *42*(2), pp. 107–139.

Jaeger, A. J., Tuchmayer, J. B. and Morin, S. M. (2014). The engaged dissertation: Exploring trends in doctoral student research. *Journal of Higher Education Outreach and Engagement*, *18*(4), pp.71–96.

Jamieson, K. H., Kahan, D. and Scheufele, D. A. Eds., 2017. *The Oxford handbook of the science of science communication*. Oxford University Press. pp.14031–14032.

Janssen, F. J. J. M. and Van Berkel, B., 2015. Making philosophy of science education practical for science teachers. *Science & Education*, *24*, pp.229–258.

Jasanoff, Sheila, Markle, G. E., Peterson, J. C. and Pinch, T. Eds., 2001. *Handbook of science and technology studies*. Sage.

Jensen, E. A. and Gerber, A., 2020. Evidence-based science communication. *Frontiers in Communication*, *4*, p.513449.

Kahan, D. M., 2015. What is the "Science of Science Communication?" *Journal of Science Communication*, *14*(3), pp.1–10.

Kahan, D. M., 2017. "Ordinary science intelligence": A science-comprehension measure for study of risk and science communication, with notes on evolution and climate change. *Journal of Risk Research*, *20*(8), pp.995–1016.

Kahan, D. M., Jenkins-Smith, H. and Braman, D., 2011. Cultural cognition of scientific consensus. *Journal of Risk Research*, *14*(2), pp.147–174.

Kampourakis, K., 2022 Reconsidering the goals of evolution education: Defining *evolution* and *evolutionary* literacy. *Evolution: Education and Outreach*, *15*(21), p. 21.

Kayumova, S. and Dou, R., 2022. Equity and justice in science education: Toward a pluriverse of multiple identities and onto-epistemologies. *Science Education*, *106*(5), pp.1097–1117.

Keiler, L. S., 2018. Teachers' roles and identities in student-centered classrooms. *International Journal of STEM Education*, *5*, pp.1–20.

Keren, A., 2018. The public understanding of what? Laypersons' epistemic needs, the division of cognitive labor, and the demarcation of science. *Philosophy of Science*, *85*(5), pp.781–792.

Kimbrell, E., Philippe, G. and Longshore, M. C., 2022. Scientific institutions should support inclusive engagement: Reflections on the AAAS center for public engagement approach. *Frontiers in Communication*, *6*, p.282.

Kuhn, T. S., 1962. *The structure of scientific revolutions*. University of Chicago press.

Ladson-Billings, G., 1995. Toward a theory of culturally relevant pedagogy. *American Educational Research Journal*, *32*(3), pp.465–491.

Ladson-Billings, G., 2023. "Yes, but how do we do it?": Practicing culturally relevant pedagogy. In Landsman, J., and Lewis, C. W. (Eds), *White teachers/diverse classrooms*. Routledge, pp. 33–46.

Landrum, A., 2020. "Knowledge + Identity in Acceptance of Science." Public Engagement with Science Workshop, University of Cincinnati Center for Public Engagement with Science. https://youtu.be/WrocFZCTIjc?si=_aryRec61VEpHGHh.

Lane, T. B. (2017). Beyond academic and social integration: Understanding the impact of a STEM enrichment program on the retention and degree attainment of underrepresented students. *CBE – Life Sciences Education*, *15*(39), pp.1–13. https://doi.org/10.1187/cbe.16-01-0070.

Latham, K. F. and Simmons, J. E., 2014. *Foundations of museum studies: Evolving systems of knowledge*: Evolving systems of knowledge. ABC-CLIO.

Laursen, S. L., H. Thiry, and C. S. Liston. 2012. The impact of a university-based school science outreach program on graduate student participants' career paths and professional socialization. *Journal of Higher Education Outreach and Engagement 16*(2), pp. 47–78.

Layton, D., 1993. *Inarticulate science?: Perspectives on the public understanding of science and some implications for science education.* Studies in Education.

Lewandowsky, S., Cook, J., Ecker, U. et al., 2020. The debunking handbook 2020.

Lok, C., 2010. Science for the masses: The US national science foundation's insistence that every research project addresses' broader impacts' leaves many researchers baffled. Corie Lok takes a looks at the system. *Nature 465*(7297), pp. 416–419.

Lombrozo, T., Thanukos, A. and Weisberg, M., 2008. The importance of understanding the nature of science for accepting evolution. *Evolution: Education and Outreach, 1*, pp.290–298.

Lonetree, A., 2012. *Decolonizing museums: Representing Native America in national and tribal museums.* University of North Carolina Press.

McCain, K., and K. Kampourakis. 2018. Which question do polls about evolution and belief really ask, and why does it matter?." *Public Understanding of Science 27*(1), pp. 2–10.

McCallie, E., Bell, L., Lohwater, T. et al. 2009. Many experts, many audiences: Public engagement with science and informal science education. A CAISE Inquiry Group Report. Washington, DC: Center for Advancement of Informal Science Education (CAISE). http://caise.insci.org/uploads/docs/public_engagement_with_science.pdf.

McComas, W. F. and Nouri, N., 2016. The nature of science and the next generation science standards: Analysis and critique. *Journal of Science Teacher Education, 27*(5), pp.555–576.

McCombs, B. L. and Whisler, J. S., 1997. *The Learner-Centered Classroom and School: Strategies for Increasing Student Motivation and Achievement. The Jossey-Bass Education Series.* Jossey-Bass, 350 Sansome St., San Francisco, CA 94104.

McIntyre, L., 2021. *How to talk to a science denier: Conversations with flat earthers, climate deniers, and others who defy reason.* MIT Press.

McKinley, E. and Gan, M. J., 2014. Culturally responsive science education for indigenous and ethnic minority students. *Handbook of Research on Science Education, 2*, pp.284–300.

Metz, S. E., Weisberg, D. S. and Weisberg, M., 2018. Non-scientific criteria for belief sustain counter-scientific beliefs. *Cognitive Science, 42*(5), pp.1477–1503.

Metz, S. E., Weisberg, D. S. and Weisberg, M. 2020. A case of sustained internal contradiction: Unresolved ambivalence between evolution and creationism. *Journal of Cognition and Culture 20*(3–4), pp. 338–354.

Miller, S., 2001. Public understanding of science at the crossroads. *Public Understanding of Science, 10*(1), pp.115–120.

Miller, E., Manz, E., Russ, R., Stroupe, D. and Berland, L., 2018. Addressing the epistemic elephant in the room: Epistemic agency and the next generation science standards. *Journal of Research in Science Teaching, 55*(7), pp.1053–1075.

National Academies of Sciences, Engineering, and Medicine. 2005. *Facilitating interdisciplinary research*. The National Academies Press. https://doi.org/10.17226/11153.

National Academies of Sciences, Engineering, and Medicine. 2016. *Science literacy: Concepts, contexts, and consequences*. The National Academies Press. https://doi.org/10.17226/23595.

National Academies of Sciences, Engineering, and Medicine. 2018. *Graduate STEM education for the 21st century*. The National Academies Press. http://nap.edu/25038.

National Commission for the Protection of Human Subjects of Biomedical, and Behavioral Research. United States. 1978. *The Belmont report: Ethical principles and guidelines for the protection of human subjects of research*.

National Research Council. 2006. *To recruit and advance: Women students and faculty in science and engineering*. National Academies Press.

National Research Council. 2009. *Learning science in informal environments: People, places, and pursuits*. National Academies Press. https://doi.org/10.17226/12190.

National Research Council. 2011. *Expanding underrepresented minority participation: America's science and technology talent at the crossroads*. National Academies Press.

National Research Council. 2012. *Discipline-based education research: Understanding and improving learning in undergraduate science and engineering*. The National Academies Press. https://doi.org/10.17226/13362.

National Research Council. 2013. *Seeking solutions: Maximizing American talent by advancing women of color in academia: Summary of a conference*. National Academies Press.

National Science Foundation. 2015. *Perspectives on broader impacts*. National Science Foundation NSF15-008. https://nsf-gov-resources.nsf.gov/2022-09/Broader_Impacts_0.pdf.

National Science Foundation website, https://new.nsf.gov/funding/learn/broader-impacts. Last accessed July 18, 2023.

Neurath, O. (1959). Protocol sentences. In Ayer, A. (Ed.), *Logical positivism* (pp. 199–208). Library of Philosophical Movements, 2. The Free Press.

Next Generation Science Standards. 2017. www.nextgenscience.org.

Nisbet, M. C. and Scheufele, D. A., 2009. What's next for science communication? Promising directions and lingering distractions. *American Journal of Botany*, 96(10), pp.1767–1778.

Onciul, B., 2015. *Museums, heritage and Indigenous voice: Decolonizing engagement.* Routledge.

Oreskes, N. and Conway, E. M., 2011. *Merchants of doubt: How a handful of scientists obscured the truth on issues from tobacco smoke to global warming.* Bloomsbury.

Pardo, R. and Félix C., 2004. The Cognitive Dimension of Public Perceptions of Science: Methodological Issues. *Public Understanding of Science (Bristol, England)*, 13(3), pp.203–227.

Pew Research Center, January 29, 2015, "Public and Scientists' Views on Science and Society," pp.1–100. www.pewresearch.org/internet/wp-content/uploads/sites/9/2015/01/PI_ScienceandSociety_Report_012915.pdf.

Pew Research Center, July 1, 2015, "Major Gaps between the Public, Scientists on Key Issues."

Pew Research Center, May 2021, "Gen Z, Millennials Stand Out for Climate Change Activism, Social Media Engagement with Issue", pp. 1–100. www.pewresearch.org/science/wp-content/uploads/sites/16/2021/05/PS_2021.05.26_climate-and-generations_REPORT.pdf.

Pfirman, S. and Martin, P. J., 2010. Facilitating interdisciplinary scholars. In Frodeman, R. (ed.), *The Oxford Handbook of Interdisciplinarity*, Chapter 27, pp.387–403.

Potochnik, Angela, 2024. *Science and the Public.* Elements in Philosophy of Science. Cambridge University Press.

Potochnik, A., Colombo, M. and Wright, C., 2024. *Recipes for science: An introduction to scientific methods and reasoning.* 2nd Ed. Routledge.

Rainey, K., Dancy, M., Mickelson, R., Stearns, E. and Moller, S., 2018. Race and gender differences in how sense of belonging influences decisions to major in STEM. *International Journal of STEM Education*, 5, pp.1–14.

Reincke, C. M., Bredenoord, A. L. and van Mil, M. H., 2020. From deficit to dialogue in science communication: The dialogue communication model requires additional roles from scientists. *EMBO Reports*, 21(9), p.e51278.

Richardson, S. S., 2010. Feminist philosophy of science: History, contributions, and challenges. *Synthese*, 177, pp.337–362.

Riemer, M., Reich, S., Evans, S., Nelson, G., and Prilleltensky, I., 2020. *Community psychology: In pursuit of liberation and well-being*. 3rd Ed. Springer.

Roberts, D. A. and Bybee, R. W., 2014. Scientific literacy, science literacy, and science education. In Lederman, N. G. and Abbell S. K. (Eds.), *Handbook of research on science education, Volume II* (pp. 559–572). Routledge.

Ross, L. F, Loup, A., Nelson, R. M. et al., 2010. The challenges of collaboration for academic and community partners in a research partnership: Points to consider. *Journal of Empirical Research on Human Research Ethics*, 5(1), pp.19–31.

Rudolph, John L., 2023. *Why we teach science (and why we should)*. Oxford University Press.

Schienke, E. W., Tuana, N., Brown, D. A. et al., 2009. The role of the National Science Foundation broader impacts criterion in enhancing research ethics pedagogy. *Social Epistemology*, 23(3–4), pp.317–336.

Schroeder, S. A., 2022. Thinking about values in science: Ethical versus political approaches. *Canadian Journal of Philosophy*, 52(3), pp.246–255.

Science and Technology Committee, 2023. Diversity and inclusion in STEM. Fifth Report of Session 2022–23, House of Commons.

Seethaler, S., Evans, J. H., Gere, C. and Rajagopalan, R. M., 2019. Science, values, and science communication: Competencies for pushing beyond the deficit model. *Science Communication*, 41(3), pp.378–388.

Shirk, J. L., Ballard, H. L., Wilderman, C. C. et al., 2012. Public participation in scientific research: A framework for deliberate design. *Ecology and Society*, 17(2), p.29–48.

Simis, M. J., Madden, H., Cacciatore, M. A. and Yeo, S. K., 2016. "The lure of rationality: Why does the deficit model persist in science communication?" *Public Understanding of Science*, 25(4), pp.400–414.

Sismondo, S., 2010. *An introduction to science and technology studies* (Vol. 1, pp. 1–11). Wiley-Blackwell.

Slater, M. and Scholfield, E. R. 2022. Trust of science as a public collective good. *Philosophy of Science*, 89(5), pp.1034–1043.

Smith, T., Avraamidou, L. and Adams, J. D., 2022. Culturally relevant/responsive and sustaining pedagogies in science education: Theoretical perspectives and curriculum implications. *Cultural Studies of Science Education*, 17(3), pp.637–660.

Strevens, M., 2020. *The knowledge machine: How irrationality created modern science*. Liveright.

Sturgis, P. and Allum, N., 2004. Science in society: Re-evaluating the deficit model of public attitudes. *Public Understanding of Science*, 13(1), pp.55–74.

Thevenot, Y., 2022. Culturally responsive and sustaining STEM curriculum as a problem-based science approach to supporting student achievement for Black and Latinx students. *Voices Urban Education*, *50*, pp.60–69.

Thorp, H. H., 2024. Teach philosophy of science. *Science*, *384*, p.141. https://doi.org/10.1126/science.adp7153.

Van der Linden, S., Leiserowitz, A., Rosenthal, S. and Maibach, E., 2017. Inoculating the public against misinformation about climate change. *Global Challenges*, *1*(2), p.1600008.

Vaughn, L. M. and Jacquez, F., 2020. Participatory research methods–Choice points in the research process. *Journal of Participatory Research Methods*, *1*(1), doi: https://doi.org/10.35844/001c.13244.

Weingart, P., Joubert, M. and Connoway, K., 2021. Public engagement with science – Origins, motives and impact in academic literature and science policy. *PloS one*, *16*(7), p.e0254201.

Weisberg, D. S., Landrum, A. R., Metz, S. E. and Weisberg, M., 2018. No missing link: Knowledge predicts acceptance of evolution in the United States. *BioScience*, *68*(3), pp.212–222.

Weisberg, D. S., Landrum, A. R., Hamilton, J. and Weisberg, M., 2021. Knowledge about the nature of science increases public acceptance of science regardless of identity factors. *Public Understanding of Science*, *30*(2), pp.120–138.

Wiggins, G., and "Jay McTighe. Understanding by design." 2005. *Association for Supervision and Curriculum Development.*

Wynne, B., 1991. Knowledges in context. *Science, Technology, & Human Values*, *16*(1), pp.111–121.

Young, I. M. (1990). *Justice and the Politics of Difference.* Princeton University Press.

Zhang, J., Tian, Y., Yuan, G. and Tao, D., 2022. Epistemic agency for costructuring expansive knowledge-building practices. *Science Education*, *106*(4), pp.890–923.

Ziman, J., 1991. Public understanding of science. *Science, Technology, & Human Values*, *16*(1), pp.99–105.

Acknowledgments

We are deeply grateful to our many collaborators in the University of Cincinnati Center for Public Engagement with Science (PEWS). PEWS Faculty Affiliates, Graduate Student Affiliates, and other collaborators from a wide range of disciplines have been essential to shaping our understanding of public engagement with science. This project has also been influenced by members of the PEWS Research and Discussion, or "R&D," group, including Amanda Corris, Lucas Dunlap, Andrew Evans, Tim Elmo Feiten, Collin Lucken, Eduardo Martinez, Chris Rickels, Zach Srivastava, and Kat Timm, among others. Research collaborations with Andrew Evans and Chris Rickels, including an academic presentation Andrew and Chris prepared, also contributed to Section 4's discussion of a public-centered model of engagement. Vanessa Carbonell also provided helpful input on applied ethics resources for Section 2.

Thank you as well to our Elements series editor Matt Lloyd for his patient support for the development of this series and Element, as well as to the Editorial Board of this series for your visionary leadership of this new initiative and for serving as reviewers for this Element: Kelly Joyce (Department of Sociology and the Center for Science, Technology and Society, Drexel University), Kostas Kampourakis (University Teacher Education Institute and the Section of Biology, University of Geneva), Rae Ostman (School for the Future of Innovation in Society and Center for Innovation in Informal STEM Learning, Arizona State University; Director of the National Informal STEM Education Network, or NISE Net), Luisa Massarani (Coordinator of Brazil's National Institute of Public Communication of Science and Technology; Regional Director for Latin America and the Caribbean of SciDev.net), Shobita Parthasarathy (Ford School of Public Policy, University of Michigan), and Dione Rossiter (Executive Director of Science at Cal at University of California, Berkeley). Rae Ostman deserves special thanks for serving as the guest editor for this Element.

This research was supported by NSF Conference Award SES-1946951, "Public Engagement and Philosophy of Science" (PI Melissa Jacquart), by the University of Cincinnati's Next Lives Here Research 2030 Program, and by The Island Systems Integration Consortium (ISIC), DEB-2114466 (PI Christine Parent, ISIC contact Co-PI Lucinda Lawson). Potochnik's time on the project was also supported by a Research Fellowship from the Charles Phelps Taft Research Center at the University of Cincinnati. This Element is freely available in an open access edition thanks to TOME (Toward an Open Monograph Ecosystem) – a collaboration of the Association of American Universities, the Association of University Presses, and the Association of Research Libraries – and the generous support of the University of Cincinnati.

Cambridge Elements =

Public Engagement with Science

Angela Potochnik
University of Cincinnati

Angela Potochnik is a Professor of philosophy and Director of the Center for Public Engagement with Science at the University of Cincinnati. Her research addresses the nature of science and its successes, the relationships between science and the public, and methods in population biology. She is the author of *Idealization and the Aims of Science* (Chicago, 2017), *Science and the Public* (Cambridge, 2024), and coauthor of *Recipes for Science* (Routledge, 2018), an introduction to scientific methods and reasoning.

Melissa Jacquart
University of Cincinnati

Melissa Jacquart is an Assistant Professor of philosophy and Curriculum & Pedagogy Director for the Center for Public Engagement with Science at the University of Cincinnati. Her research focuses on epistemological issues in the philosophy of science, philosophy of astrophysics, feminist philosophy, philosophy and education, and public engagement with science. She is a 2022–2023 Whiting Public Engagement Fellow.

Editorial Board
Kelly Joyce, *Drexel University*
Kostas Kampourakis, *University of Geneva*
Luisa Massarani, *SciDev.net*
Rae Ostman, *Arizona State University*
Shobita Parthasarathy, *University of Michigan*
Dione Rossiter, *University of California, Berkeley*

About the Series
This interdisciplinary series draws from a broad range of research and professional expertise to guide theory and practice of public engagement with science, including science communication, formal and informal science education, community participation in scientific research, science policy, and other interfaces between science and the public.

Cambridge Elements

Public Engagement with Science

Elements in the Series

Public Engagement with Science: Defining the Project
Angela Potochnik and Melissa Jacquart

A full series listing is available at: www.cambridge.org/PEWS

For EU product safety concerns, contact us at Calle de José Abascal, 56–1°,
28003 Madrid, Spain or eugpsr@cambridge.org.

www.ingramcontent.com/pod-product-compliance
Ingram Content Group UK Ltd.
Pitfield, Milton Keynes, MK11 3LW, UK
UKHW021925010525
458033UK00019B/347